HOLISTIC
RISK MANAGEMENT
IN PRACTICE

OTHER RISK BOOKS PUBLISHED BY WITHERBYS

Business Finance for Risk Management
Business Organisation and Finance
Corporate Risk Management
Insurance, Non Marine – An Introduction
Liability Exposures
Liability Risk and the Law
Local Government a Text for Risk Managers
Risk Control
Risk and the Business Environment
Risk Analysis
Risk Financing
Risk Management
Risk Management in Healthcare
Treasury Risk Management

British Library Cataloguing in Publication Data

Hopkin, Paul
Holistic Risk Management in Practice
1 Title
ISBN 1 85609 227 5

HOLISTIC
RISK MANAGEMENT
IN PRACTICE

Paul Hopkin

First Edition 2002

WITHERBY

PUBLISHERS

© Paul Hopkin

2002

ISBN 1 85609 227 5

Printed and Published by
WITHERBY & CO. LTD
32-36 Aylesbury Street
London EC1R 0ET
Tel No: 020 7251 5341   Fax No: 020 7251 1296
International Tel No: +44 20 7251 5341
International Fax No: +44 20 7251 1296
E-mail: books@witherbys.co.uk
www: witherbys.com

Foreword

Despite the fact that there has been a lot of talk (and that's largely what it is) about risk management in recent years, there haven't been many books or indeed any that add much to the literature on risk management from its intellectual heyday of the 1970's and 1980's.

Discussion about risk management has focused on descriptions and title, e.g. enterprise risk management, holistic risk management, integrated risk management and the Chief Risk Officer, with very little emphasis on action and how to do it in a practical way.

I suggest this is because risk management publicity has fallen into the hands of non-practitioners, e.g. consultants, accountants, lawyers and insurance brokers who see the recent fashion for corporate governance (which itself looks a somewhat pathetic concept in the light of what has gone on in a number of well publicised corporate disasters) and what this might produce in new revenues.

Historically practitioners have not, since the days of Douglas Barlow, written much about risk management and rarely share their practical experience of assisting with managing risk within their corporations.

A concept or business process described by consultants but not supported convincingly by practical and demonstrably successful practice is worthless and is one reason why risk management does not have the credibility it should have.

Paul Hopkin has been and indeed is a practitioner and unlike many of his peers comes not from an insurance but a loss control background – an essential distinction if one is to concentrate on managing risk to its full extent.

He has also worked for demanding businesses and in one case where I worked with him (yes wearing a non-practising consultancy hat), he not only helped to get the message across to sceptical and profit orientated businessmen but developed a methodology where risk management success or failure was built into both corporate and individual performance.

This book reflects this experience and is consequently of value to all concerned with practical risk management. Although wordy this is balanced by the clever idea of including a summary of the author's views at the end of each chapter and all combined in a full chapter at the end. Indeed this summary might benefit from being separately published as an Executive summary or monograph or perhaps in future editions become a valuable Preface.

There are many pearls of wisdom in these summaries and Paul Hopkin might reflect on the fact that he can get his message across extremely well in fewer words than he thinks. However, the repetition and ongoing summaries do have the advantage of getting across his message clearly and strongly.

He introduces new definitions and initials for the concepts he describes. Many are improvements on the old ones.

I like the idea of GRASP (Guardian of the Risk Architecture, Strategy and Protocols) to describe the role of the risk manager and the term 'Risk Assurance' to describe the system of managing risk and 'Risk Response' to describe loss control strategies.

I am less keen on NUDE (No Unplanned Dysfunctional Events) which seems derived from a desire to find words to fit the acronym rather than to explain the concept. This is a quibble and there is no better quibble or low marker than myself.

Each section of the book includes an excellent and accessible case study – using as examples a football club, theatre, publisher, personal life, the author gets across his message clearly and students will find the combination of erudition, experience, clear summaries and realistic case studies extremely helpful.

Risk management has had an eventful life over the last 30 to 40 years – in the early days it came out of both an academic and practical background which produced many good publications (most of which have stood the test of time), it then got shanghaied by the insurance industry and become far too focused on risk financing, captives etc. More recently it has become pretentious, somewhat hollow with little to offer a dynamic and realistic business enterprise.

I hope this book will complete the circle and restore the balance. It deserves to because it focuses on how risk management can contribute to making a business successful. It addresses the need for a practical approach which can be fully understood and communicated throughout the organisation.

It is not pessimistic about risk, the opportunities that can arise are dealt with and the importance of taking risk to improve value – which is often ignored by risk managers despite the fact that managers do this all the time – is emphasised and built into the methodologies that Paul Hopkin presents to us.

The patient and open-minded reader will get value from this book.

Paul Bawcutt
March 2002

Preface

What is planned as strategic or integrative risk management must not degenerate into (or revert to) operational risk response

Stakeholders demand continuous improvement in performance. Each time a customer buys a new car, he or she expects it to be better than the previous model. This expectation of continuous improvement in performance places additional demands on organisations. These demands result in organisations needing to achieve necessary and appropriate standards of leadership, competition and efficiency, and the need for continuous evaluation and constant change is thus implied.

Constant change creates risks that have to be managed. It is worth noting that more time taken in making a decision allows more information to be collected, however fewer viable options will then remain. Risk management is the initiative of the moment; because it facilitates robust decision-making. In these days of constant change, decisions need to be taken more rapidly. So that risk management can assist with the rapid making of decisions, the various historical approaches to the discipline of risk management need to be brought together and co-ordinated into an effective approach for the future. This "new way forward" must acknowledge the contributions of the past and develop the approaches for the future.

"Holistic Risk Management" is a phrase frequently used to describe a particular approach to the management of corporate or business risks. A better description would be the phrase "Holistic Risk Management". The word integrative implies a more dynamic forward thinking rather than a task that was done in the past and is now complete. Risk management should be predictive, creative and exhaustive, not predicted, created and exhausted.

Several other words are also used to describe the concept of "Holistic Risk Management". These words or phrases include aligned, embedded, strategic, business and 'total enterprise'. Although it is often difficult to agree terminology, the underlying approach is consistent. This book explores the benefits of the different approaches and seeks to identify the ways in which these ideas can be used to build a fully integrative risk management model.

If the integrative risk management approach is to be successful, it must find the answer to the question "what should the organisation do about the significant risks that could impact achievement of the corporate mission?". This requires the identification and evaluation of all potentially significant risks and the treatment, monitoring and review of the priority significant risks faced by the organisation.

This approach requires the organisation to identify all of the potentially significant risks, regardless of historical approaches and existing arrangements. The distinctions, insurable or uninsurable, pure or speculative, internal or external, controllable or uncontrollable all hinder an integrative risk management exercise.

This book examines the current status of the discipline of risk management and the contribution that risk management tools and techniques can make to the fulfilment of the corporate mission. Risk management currently faces many challenging questions and it is not yet proven that "Holistic Risk Management" will be able to deliver all of the benefits that have been promised by risk management specialists, practitioners and consultants.

The fact that risk management is currently a high profile management initiative means that it has become fashionable. Fashion is dangerous in this context, because what is fashionable becomes highly desirable. However, what is fashionable today will, in time, become very unfashionable. The result will be that risk management as a valuable discipline becomes discredited.

For those who have experience in risk management, it is strange to find that their discipline is suddenly high profile and everybody claims to be an expert. At the moment, everybody wants to control the risk management agenda. It is important that the risk manager becomes the voice of reason and experience. Part of the task of the risk manager is to ensure that the discipline does not exaggerate the contribution it can make or overstate the scope of application of risk management. Making exaggerated claims will increase the chances of the discipline of risk management becoming discredited.

The ideas and concepts discussed in this book are more fully explored and applied in the consolidated case study set out in Appendix B. Note that the ideas are, to some extent, empirical and the concepts are still being developed. Indeed, the discipline itself is currently going though an exciting phase of transfer from empirical theory to established practice. It will continue to develop until (at least) the middle of the first decade of this century. Risk Management has strong origins related to hazards and hazard management. Many of the examples used in this book are based on hazard risks and hazard management. The ideas and principles put forward are, however, equally applicable to control risks and opportunity risks.

This book is intended to add to the debate on the contribution that risk management can make to the success of an organisation. The aim of all risk management practitioners is to ensure that the discipline continues to contribute to the achievement of the corporate mission. This contribution will only be valued if risk management facilitates a sustained increase in the level of success of the organisation.

Paul Hopkin

April 2002

Acknowledgements

The author is grateful to all of his friends and colleagues who have contributed to the thought processes that lay behind this book. He is grateful, in particular, to Anna Nicholl, Risk Manager at Mellon Global Investments, for her critique of the book. Her comments and observations have added considerably to the clarity of expression.

The author acknowledges his thanks, in advance, to the individuals who will offer their thoughts and observations on the ideas put forward in this book. The importance of managing risks will increase in the years to come and it is by sharing ideas that the discipline will develop. Provided that we respond to the views of all those who have an interest in risk management, then the simple act of sharing risk approaches and risk agendas will, of itself, contribute to the improved management of risks.

The Author

Paul Hopkin BSc, FIIRSM, FIOSH, FIRM is based in London as the Director of Risk Management for The Rank Group Plc. He was previously Head of Risk Management at the BBC. A former HM Inspector of Factories with the Health and Safety Executive, he is a Fellow of the International Institute of Risk and Safety Management, as well as the Institute of Risk Management and the Institution of Occupational Safety and Health.

Paul has recently become a member of the Board of the International Institute of Risk and Safety Management (IIRSM). He is also a former Deputy Chairman of the Association of Insurance and Risk Managers (AIRMIC). Paul is a former chair of the Risk Management Special Interest Group of the Strategic Planning Society.

Paul previously held the positions of Loss Control Manager at BET plc, Technical Director at Sedgwick Risk Control Services, Managing Director of Fenchurch Risk Management and Director of Richard Oliver International, part of the Willis (Insurance Brokers) Group. For four years he ran his own consultancy specialising in risk assessment and safety management.

Contents

List of Figures

List of Tables

Part 1

INTRODUCTION TO RISK

1 NATURE OF RISK

Do not manage risks out of context, or in isolation from the situation that gave rise to the risk initially

This chapter offers a comprehensive definition of risk. The nature of risk is considered in relation to the achievement of the corporate mission. In addition, the importance of corporate objectives, stakeholder expectations, core processes and key dependencies are explained in terms of the impact that risks could have on the organisation.

Risk can be defined as a circumstance, action, situation or event (CASE) with the ability or potential to impact the key dependencies that support the core processes of the organisation. Core processes are designed to fulfil corporate objectives and deliver stakeholder expectations. The core processes, corporate objectives and stakeholder expectations underpin the mission of the organisation. The impact of a risk on the key dependencies could be to enhance achievement of the mission, inhibit achievement of the mission or cause doubt about whether the mission will be achieved. The risks that can enhance, inhibit and cause doubt are referred to as opportunity risks, hazard risks and control risks.

There is a tendency for risk management specialists to adopt approaches that result in the separation of risks from the situation that gave rise to those risks. Risk is an integral part of corporate activity and risks should not be managed out of context or in isolation from the situation that gave rise to them. By managing risks in context, risk management will become a dynamic activity. Paying regard to risks and risk management should become an integral part of decision making.

1.1 Definition of Risk

Many different definitions of risk have been devised, depending on the context used and the background of the person proposing the definition. In order to avoid confusion, a standard and clearly understood definition is needed. The definition set out below is very general and it is also explored more fully in later chapters. It is useful to have an extensive and all-inclusive definition of risk, so that all interested parties can agree the scope of risk management. The following definition of a risk is used in this book:

A **circumstance, action, situation or event** (1) with the ability or potential to **impact** (2) the **key dependencies** (3) that support the **core processes** (4) of the organisation.

Defining a hierarchy of management imperatives for the organisation can further clarify the definition. The mission is the ultimate imperative, followed by the corporate objectives and the stakeholder expectations. The core processes within the organisation deliver the mission, corporate objectives and stakeholder expectations. Key dependencies support the core processes and risks can impact these key dependencies. The risks can enhance, inhibit or cause doubt about the availability or performance of a key dependency. Figure 1 (p6) provides a graphical representation of this hierarchy of management imperatives.

In order to assist with the understanding of the ideas put forward in this book, a common language and understanding of risk is required. Appendix A sets out definitions and terminology, including the fundamentally important definition of core process. Risk now has a broader meaning within the business community than used to be the case. It is no longer true that risks are only associated with adverse outcomes and downside events. A risk can inhibit, enhance or cause doubt about the achievement of the mission of the organisation. It is useful to consider the definition in more detail, by exploring the numbered sections of the definition set out above.

(1) **circumstance, action, situation or event.** A risk is (or is associated with) a "circumstance, action, situation or event" (or CASE) with the potential to impact the mission of the organisation. Greater competition in the marketplace, for example, is not sufficiently specific to be considered as a risk. When stated in such general terms it becomes a management issue. It is only when competitors

undertake an action, create an event, bring about a circumstance or produce a situation that a risk has materialised. Although it is too narrow to serve as a full definition, it is sometimes helpful to consider that a risk must be an event. Acceptance that a risk must be a CASE helps when a list or matrix of possible risks is being produced. Risks will be better defined if each potential risk is defined and described as a circumstance, action, situation or event.

(2) **impact.** Impact is used in the definition to reinforce the idea that risks are not always bad. The impact could be negative, positive or uncertain. Some CASE will inhibit the mission (hazards or hazard risks), some will enhance the mission (opportunities or opportunity risks) and others will cause doubt about achieving the mission (uncertainties or control risks).

(3) **key dependencies.** Key dependencies must be present if the core processes are to continue successfully. They are associated with the financial, infrastructure, reputational and/or the marketplace components that must be present if the core processes are to be sustained. Key dependencies are vital if the organisation is going to achieve the mission, corporate objectives and stakeholder expectations. Key dependencies support the core processes, as illustrated in Figure 1 overleaf.

(4) **core processes.** A core process is fundamental to the continued success (or even existence in its present size and form) of the organisation and the ability to achieve the corporate mission. Each core process creates value in the organisation and delivers one or more stakeholder expectation. There are three basic types of core processes. These are processes for the:

- continuity and monitoring of routine operations

- management of projects and enhancements

- development and delivery of strategy

Processes are made up of activities. An activity is an individual job or task undertaken within the organisation. These related and inter-dependent activities build to make processes. Each additional activity adds cost to the process, although the intention of each activity is to make the process more robust.

Figure 1 also illustrates the context within which risks arise; the relationship between the mission, corporate objectives, stakeholder expectations and core processes. The nature of corporate objectives, stakeholder expectations and core processes is explored in more detail below.

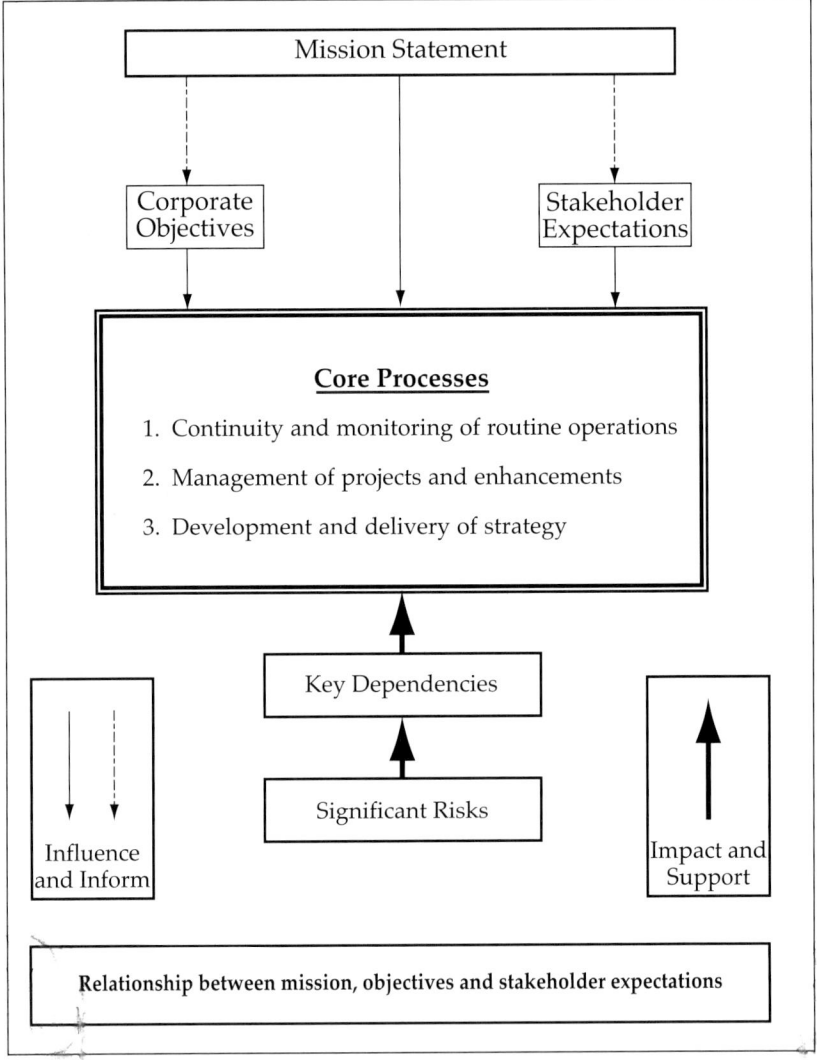

Figure 1: Risks in Context

1.1.1 Corporate Objectives

Consideration of corporate objectives adds to the understanding of the context within which risks arise. The most commonly used definition of risk describes risks as "anything that can impact fulfilment of corporate objectives" but for the reasons discussed below, this definition is considered to be too narrow. Nevertheless, it remains true that no systematic approach to risk can be complete without a consideration of corporate objectives.

A difficulty with risk being defined as "anything that can impact fulfilment of corporate objectives" is that those objectives are not fully stated by most organisations. Where objectives have been established, they tend to be stated as internal, annual, change objectives. This is particularly true of the personal objectives of members of staff in the organisation.

It is clearly the case that risks are greater in circumstances of change. Therefore, linking risks to change objectives is not illogical or unreasonable, but analysis of each objective may not lead to robust risk identification. Objectives are usually stated at too high a level for the successful attachment of risks. To be useful to the organisation, the corporate objectives should be presented as a full statement of the short, medium and long term aims of the organisation. Internal, annual, change objectives are usually inadequate, because they may fail to fully identify the operational (or efficiency), change (or competition) and strategic (or leadership), requirements of the organisation.

The most important disadvantage associated with the "objectives-driven" approach is the danger of considering risks out of the context that gave rise to them. Risks that are analysed in a way that is separated from the situation that gave rise to them, because they are attached to high level corporate objectives, will not be capable of rigorous and informed evaluation. A more robust analysis will be achieved by a "dependencies-driven" approach to risk management.

It remains the case that many organisations continue to use analysis of corporate objectives as a means of identifying risks, as benefits do arise from this approach. For example, using the "objectives-driven" approach facilitates the analysis of risks in relation to the positive and uncertain aspects of the CASE that may occur, as well as facilitating the analysis of the negative aspects.

1.1.2   Stakeholder Expectations

All organisations have a range of stakeholders and these stakeholders can be internal or external to the organisation. Some of the stakeholders may be unwelcome, such as pressure groups that target a particular aspect of what they consider to be ethical behaviour. The organisation will often be obligated to respond to these (perhaps unwanted) expectations. An example of such unwanted stakeholders is the environmental pressure groups that have expectations of, (say), a chemical company.

To obtain the fullest picture of the risks facing an organisation, analysis of stakeholders and their expectations is necessary. The identification of stakeholder expectations is the output from the external evaluation stage of the business cycle as discussed in a later chapter. A stakeholder expectation is a requirement that the stakeholder has of the organisation. Different stakeholders may have expectations that are contradictory or even mutually exclusive in terms of the demands placed on the organisation.

Core processes deliver stakeholder expectations. A risk can be defined as a circumstance, action, situation or event (CASE) with the potential to impact the fulfilment of a stakeholder expectation. This approach has the advantage that both internal and external stakeholders can be identified, together with their short, medium and long term expectations.

The approach based on stakeholder expectations has many advantages. It facilitates a full and thorough validation of the core processes of the organisation in relation to the expectations that each stakeholder places on each core process. Remember that different groups of stakeholders can often have contradictory expectations e.g. members of staff are stakeholders in the organisation for which they work. A typical expectation for members of staff in most organisations is that they are financially well rewarded. This expectation will be in opposition to the expectations of the owners, or shareholders, who will be looking to achieve maximum profits.

An important aspect of managing an organisation is the balancing of the various stakeholder expectations. There are dangers inherent in achieving this balance. A risk identification process based on analysis of stakeholder expectations is the most robust way of ensuring that these dangers are recognised, analysed and then minimised.

The analysis of stakeholder expectations is also one of the fundamental requirements of the business process redesign (BPR) approach. Once the stakeholders in the future of the organisation have been identified then the expectations of each stakeholder in relation to each stated objective and the corporate mission can be evaluated. Shared expectations will emerge and the core processes of the organisation can then be defined (or refined) specifically in terms of the delivery of these shared expectations.

Although the analysis of stakeholder expectations is the most robust way of identifying risks, there are implications in terms of the time and effort required.

1.1.3   Core Processes

A process in this context, is a co-ordinated and interdependent set of activities that add value by delivering one or more stakeholder expectation. Sometimes different stakeholders will have different expectations of the same core process. It will be for management to decide the level of performance that the process will deliver. Many processes are fundamental to the continued existence of the organisation in its present size and form. These processes are the core processes of the organisation.

A core process is critical to the continued success (or even existence) of the organisation and the ability of the organisation to achieve the corporate mission and fulfil the corporate objectives. There are three basic types of core process which are for the:

- continuity and monitoring of routine operations
- management of projects and enhancements
- development and delivery of strategy

1. **continuity and monitoring of routine operations.** These are the processes designed to ensure the continuity and efficiency of routine operations. They must include explicit consideration of the risks associated with the normal, routine operations of the organisation.

2. **management of projects and enhancements.** These are the processes by which projects and other enhancements are managed and may involve project review meetings. They must include

explicit assessment and evaluation of the risks associated with the project.

3. **development and delivery of strategy.** These are the processes by which strategy is developed and delivered and may involve a sub-committee of the board, or even the board itself. They must include explicit consideration of the risks associated with each of the strategies under consideration.

Note that processes add value to the organisation by delivering stakeholder expectations. The individual activities within each process add cost, although the ultimate intention of each individual activity is, of course, to enable the process to deliver greater value.

1.2. Types of Risk

A common language of risk is required throughout the organisation, if it is to maximise the contribution of risk management. This will also enable the organisation to develop an agreed perception of risk. Part of developing this common language and perception of risk is to agree a risk classification system or series of risk classification systems.

Risks can be divided into three types or categories of risk. These three types of risk are related and (sometimes) inter-dependent. Definitions of these three types of risk are also set out in Appendix A. They are:

1. **Hazard Risks;**

2. **Control Risks; and**

3. **Opportunity Risks**

hazard risks. These are the CASE that can only inhibit achievement of the corporate mission. Typically these are insurable type risks or perils and will include fire, storm, flood, injury etc. The discipline of risk management has strong origins in the management and control of hazard risks.

control risks. These are the CASE that cause doubt about the ability of the organisation to achieve the mission. Internal financial control protocols are a good example of a response to a control risk. If the control protocols are removed then there is no way of being certain what will happen. Control risks are the most difficult type of risk to describe, but later sections of this book will assist with their understanding.

opportunity risks. These are the CASE that are often deliberately accepted by the organisation. These risks are pursued by the organisation in order to enhance the achievement of the mission, although they can sometimes inhibit the achievement of the mission, if the outcome is adverse. This is the most important type of risk for the future success of any organisation.

Several issues arise from the acknowledgement that risks can be divided into hazard risks, control risks and opportunity risks. The division implies that the approach to all three types of risk should be compatible, in terms of the attitude to values at risk. For example, it may not be consistent for an organisation to be willing to risk £5 million on an investment (opportunity risk), whilst being unwilling to accept more than £500 as excess on the motor insurance policy (hazard risk). These apparent inconsistencies are justifiable in certain circumstances, as discussed later in this chapter.

There is much written about the so-called "up-side of risk". There is a temptation amongst those concerned with hazard risks to consider that losing £2 million, when expected (or were even willing) to lose £5 million is a profit of £3 million. This approach is not helpful when considering the difference between hazard risks and opportunity risks. A hazard can only go wrong, so identifying a loss of £2 million as profit is wrong. An opportunity is taken because it is anticipated that it will deliver a net profit, despite the fact that it could, in the wrong circumstances, deliver a loss.

Note that a risk can be one type in certain circumstances but another type when those circumstances change. Risks change from one type to another within the organisation dependent on circumstances. In certain circumstances, an opportunity risk may become a control risk or even a hazard risk. Insurance companies are in the business of risk and accept the risks of other organisations for payment of a premium. In recent times, some insurance companies have faced difficulties and they have only been willing to accept certain types of business on strictly controlled terms. The risks that were previously accepted as opportunity risks have become control risks and, if claims experience deteriorates, the insurance company may come to view certain risks as hazard risks, these will then be refused altogether.

1.2.1   Hazard Risks

Organisations face a wide range of risks, those which can only go wrong are classified as hazard risks and sometimes referred to as pure risks. They may also be thought of as (substantially) operational risks or insurable risks. Organisations can be said to have a certain level of tolerance to hazard risks. The total value at risk that the organisation is willing to accept in relation to the hazard risks component of the overall risk capacity of the organisation is the hazard tolerance. The hazard tolerance is the maximum cost that the organisation is willing to tolerate by way of losses from hazard risks.

For example, an organisation may be willing to tolerate the situation where hazard risks will cost £5 million per annum. Hazard risks are, by and large undesirable but usually integral to the processes and activities within the organisation. A transport company will face a considerable range of hazard risks associated with a fleet of vehicles. For example, vehicles can break down or be stolen. Successful management of hazard risks will minimise what is sometimes referred to as the "Total Cost of Risk".

Hazard risks are measured by recording how often undesirable events occur. These measurements are equivalent to using criteria of failure. Examples of hazard risks include fire, flood, theft, accident, etc. There is close direct correlation between hazard risks and the issues that will prevent normal operation and/or introduce dysfunctional operation into the organisation.

Hazard risks must be managed within the context of managing the organisation and they should be an integral part of the responsibilities of each manager. Clearly it is not for the risk manager to become involved in the day-to-day management of hazard risks. The responsibility must belong to the appropriate manager and these risks should not be separated from the situation that gave rise to them. It is the role of the risk manager to facilitate improved management of hazard risks.

The desired state in relation to hazard risks is that of "No Unplanned Dysfunctional Events" (NUDE). Normal efficient operation may be disrupted by loss, damage, breakdown, theft etc and associated with a wide range of dependencies, including:

- property
- assets
- standards
- continuity
- people
- products

Table 1 provides a typical checklist of dependencies that must be in place for the organisation to achieve the state of NUDE. The main examples of how dysfunction could occur in relation to each dependency are also set out in Table 1.

Typical range of circumstances that can give rise to dysfunction	
NUDE Dependency	**Examples of Dysfunction**
Property	• Inadequate or insufficient property • Denial of access to property • Damage to or contamination of property
Assets	• Accidental damage to physical assets • Breakdown of plant or equipment • Theft or loss of physical assets
Standards	• Failure to ensure legal compliance • Incorrect competition and trading practices • Business ethics and employment practices
Continuity	• Inadequate management of information • Failure of internal communications • Disruption caused by third party failure
People	• Lack of people skills and/or resources • Unexpected absence of key personnel • Ill-health, accident or injury to people
Products	• Poor product or performance standards • Product liability problems and claims • Product violation or contamination

Table 1: NUDE Categories

1.2.2   Control Risks

These are risks that cause doubt or uncertainty about the ability of the organization to achieve its' mission. Control risks are the risks most akin to the area of operation of internal auditors. Organisations will be aware of the costs associated with the need to manage control risks, many organisations will accept these costs unwillingly. The costs associated with the management of control risks can be described as control acceptance. Most organisations accept the costs attached to complying with (for example) equal opportunities legislation. Control Acceptance represents the maximum expenditure that the organisation is willing to sanction in order to reduce the doubt associated with control risks, to below the acceptable level.

The current level of risk associated with a control risk may be such that spending more money on controls would be cost effective and as this expenditure will show a positive return. Again, this should not be considered to be the "up-side of risk". It is simply cost effective allocation of corporate resources.

Control Risks are associated with a criteria of uncertainly, examples include the potential for legal non-compliance and losses caused by fraud. They are usually dependent on the successful management of people and successful implementation of control protocols. Although most organisations ensure that control risks are carefully managed, they may remain potentially significant.

Control risks may be considered to relate to the management of what are sometimes called "risk factors" or "contra-indications". Using a personal lifestyle example, if you allow your weight to increase you may be at greater risk of health problems. Keeping your weight under control, thereby controlling one of the risk factors, will reduce the chances of a heart attack. There will always remain a chance of heart disease, but you have reduced the chances and made an unacceptable outcome less likely, thereby reducing doubt or uncertainty. The control acceptance in this case is the effort, time and money allocated to the ongoing control of weight.

The management of control risks makes a major contribution to project management. In overall terms, hazard risks are risks **to** the project, control risks are risks **in** the project and opportunity risks are risks **of** the project. The place of risk management in projects is considered in more detail in Chapter 4. A key component of control management, in the context of project risk management, is ensuring that the specification for the project is actually capable of delivering the required performance of the finished enhancement.

Control risks tend to be reduced to below the level of significance in an organisation and sometimes well beyond that level. Therefore it is unlikely that many control risks will emerge as priority risks that require additional control measures. Nevertheless, the management of control risks by local management, the careful monitoring of performance by senior managers and the detailed review of control risks (usually by internal auditors) are all essential.

1.2.3 Opportunity Risks

Some risks are deliberately taken by the organisation in order to achieve, or even exceed, the mission. These risks are often marketplace or commercial risks that have been taken in order to achieve a positive return. Opportunity risks can otherwise be referred to as commercial, speculative or business risks. Opportunity risks are risks with potential to enhance (although they can also inhibit) the achievement of the mission of the organisation. These risks may also be considered to be the risks associated with taking advantage of business opportunities.

Many organisations are willing to embrace high risk business strategies in anticipation of a high profit or return. These organisations may be considered to have a large opportunity appetite. Often, the same organisation will have the opposite approach to hazards risks and have a small hazard tolerance. This may be sensible; if the attitude of the organisation is that it does not want hazard related CASE consuming corporate resources, when it is putting so much value at risk in relation to opportunities. The allocation of risk capacity however should be undertaken in a way that acknowledges that risk is a single transferable commodity.

Organisations will have an appetite for opportunity risks. Opportunity appetite is the maximum resource that the organisation is willing to put at risk to take advantage of perceived opportunities. It is a component of the overall risk capacity of the organisation. Opportunity risks will usually be measured in terms of the commercial success that has been achieved. For example, the desired state on a new product development costing £5 million may be an overall profit of between £10 million and £12 million. In other words, opportunity risks are planned and evaluated in terms of criteria of success.

1.3.   Risk Exposure

Risk Capacity is the sum of the hazard tolerance, control acceptance and opportunity appetite of the organisation. It may not always be calculated or even recognised by the organisation. It represents the total resources that the organisation wishes to allocate to risk. Organisations allocate corporate resources to the following:

- reserves (or reserve funds);

- revenue (or routine expenditure);

- risk (or risk exposure)

Almost by definition, the reserves and reserve funds should not normally be put at risk by the organisation. Revenue, including routine expenditure, is associated with the planned, routine operations of the organisation. Risk exposure is the total value at risk for the organisation across the whole range of hazard risks, control risks and opportunity risks. The organisation, however, may have placed more of its resources at risk than the board realises or desires. The risk exposure is the total sum at risk in relation to the values associated with individual risks. Note that the risk exposure is a snapshot in time of the cumulative total of the actual values at risk. The risk capacity of the organisation is the maximum corporate resources that the board wishes to have at risk. These may not be the same and so the organisation needs to be satisfied that it has the appropriate risk exposure, which will be equal to the agreed risk capacity.

An organisation may be willing to, and/or believe that it is necessary to, put 25% of its total resources at risk. This amount will, of course, vary with business sector and marketplace conditions. Generally speaking, as the marketplace becomes more volatile, the organisation will be forced to increase its risk exposure. This requires a discussion in the boardroom leading to an agreement to increase the total value that the organisation is willing to put at risk and/or find mechanisms to reduce risk exposure. This explains why risk management becomes more important in times of rapid change and increased market volatility.

Risk exposure is the actual cumulative total at risk. It is calculated on a risk by risk basis, without consideration of whether the risks are correlated. An organisation will need to allow for the correlation of risks and thereby take account of the likelihood of the risks materialising. This is a sophisticated analysis, but it is the basis for an organisation being able to accept an unadjusted risk exposure that is higher than the risk capacity. This can be accepted, because the likelihood of all of the risks materialising at once (or in the same year) is low. When calculating the total actual risk exposure of the organisation, it is vitally important that the cumulative total of the values at risk is adjusted to take account of whether risks are correlated. The adjusted total risk exposure should ideally be the same as the risk capacity of the organisation.

Summary and Review of Chapter 1

Section 1 sets out some of the basic issues for consideration in defining risk. Risks can affect achievement of the mission by impacting the key dependencies that ensure fulfilment of the corporate objectives, delivery of stakeholder expectations and success of the core processes. There is a hierarchy of management imperatives for the organisation from mission to corporate objectives to stakeholder expectations to core processes.

It is important to recognise the full extent of the definition of risk so that a fully integrative approach can be developed within the organisation. If the full definition is too broad the organisation can simply apply the level of sophistication that is specific to the culture of the organisation.

Section 2 examines the historical differentiation between the management of hazard risks, control risks and opportunity risks. It is suggested that the different types of risks are related and can be analysed in a way that enables the total risk exposure of the organisation to be identified. This risk exposure can then be compared with the agreed risk capacity of the organisation.

All types of risk will be present in an organisation and the different types of risk may require different responses. These responses can be consolidated into an overall approach that works for the organisation. This will provide an opportunity for the organisation to develop an overall methodology that includes all managers and staff, as well as all risk professionals. This will be the integrative approach.

The main message from this chapter is that risks should not be separated from the situation that gave rise to the risks. The approach that should be applied to any specific risk should pick the best from the hazard, control and opportunity styles. Case Study 1 consolidates the key messages outlined in this chapter.

Case Study 1: Premiership Football Club (Part 1)

Whitechapel Football Club (Whitechapel FC) is a highly successful Premiership Football Club. Analysis of the mission, corporate objectives and stakeholder expectations will lead to the identification of the core processes for Whitechapel FC. Football fans are one of the main groups of stakeholders. They expect success on the pitch over everything else. Naturally this expectation is shared, to a greater or lesser extent, with all other stakeholders. This means that one of the most important processes for the club is "deliver successful results on the pitch". The Director of Football has overall responsibility for this core process.

The "deliver successful results on the pitch" core process has several key dependencies that must be in place if the process is to deliver the required level of success. The Director of Football is responsible for managing the outcomes of the circumstances, activities, situations and events (CASE) that could impact upon these key dependencies.

Analysis of each key dependency in turn will allow identification of the risks. These risks can be classified as hazard risks, control risks and opportunity risks and are likely to include the following:

Hazard:	— key player suffers injury before match
	— player sent off during match
Control:	— opponents adopt unexpected tactics
	— player fitness and/or stamina inadequate
Opportunity:	— purchase of new players approved
	— new team tactics to be introduced

There will be other risks and it will be for the Director of Football and his coaching team to recognise and manage all significant risks. When the significant risks have been identified, the team manager and the coaching staff will be responsible for managing and monitoring the significant risks. Management of the risks should be aligned with the mission of Whitechapel FC and the management of the risks should be embedded with other aspects of managing the team and the club. The Director of Football is responsible for the core process and managers and/or coaches will be responsible for the individual key dependencies and the associated risks.

2 Nature of Risk Management

Risk Management improves the management of the core processes of the organisation by optimising risk outcomes

This chapter considers the nature of risk management and the established stages that build the risk management discipline. Historically the term risk management has been used to describe an approach that was applied only to hazard risks. The discipline is now developing in a way that will enable risk management to make a contribution to the improved management of control risks and opportunity risks.

Risk management has well established and recognised stages that are followed when applying the discipline. These stages build into valuable risk management activities, each of which makes an important contribution. The activities associated with risk management are as follows:

- risk assessment;
- risk control;
- risk resourcing;
- event management; and
- risk assurance

Risk management can improve management of the core processes, in the organisation, by ensuring that key dependencies are analysed, monitored and reviewed. Risk management tools and techniques will assist with the management of the hazard, control and opportunity risks that could impact these key dependencies.

2.1. Risk Management Discipline

It is important to decide exactly what risk management is seeking to deliver. In simple terms, risk management is about managing and optimising the outcomes of any circumstance, action, situation or event (CASE) that materialises. At present risk management is a high profile initiative that promises many benefits. This book describes the tools and techniques of risk management that can be aligned with, and embedded into, normal management activities.

Before considering what risk management can deliver to the organisation, it is worth discussing the nature of risk management. The following have been suggested as descriptions of the nature of risk management:

- a profession or a discipline
- a set of tools and techniques
- an activity or series of activities
- a set of structured stages
- an approach or application

Risk management is a related and inter-dependent set of tools and techniques that, when applied in a structured manner, constitute a robust discipline. Risk management can be seen as both a discipline and a profession, because a discipline is a system of rules for behaviour and a profession is an occupation requiring specific training. Risk management requires specific training in the tools and techniques required to undertake and/or co-ordinate the stages in the theory and practice of the discipline. The risk management discipline has several stages and outputs.

Figure 2 illustrates the relationship between the stages that make up the risk management discipline. The stages are as follows:

1. **Recognition** or identification of risks and identification of whether the nature of the risk is hazard, control or opportunity

2. **Ranking** or evaluation of risks in terms of magnitude and likelihood, to produce the "Risk Profile" of the organisation

3. **Reassurance of Control** of risks, giving rise to an adequate level of confidence in the current controls

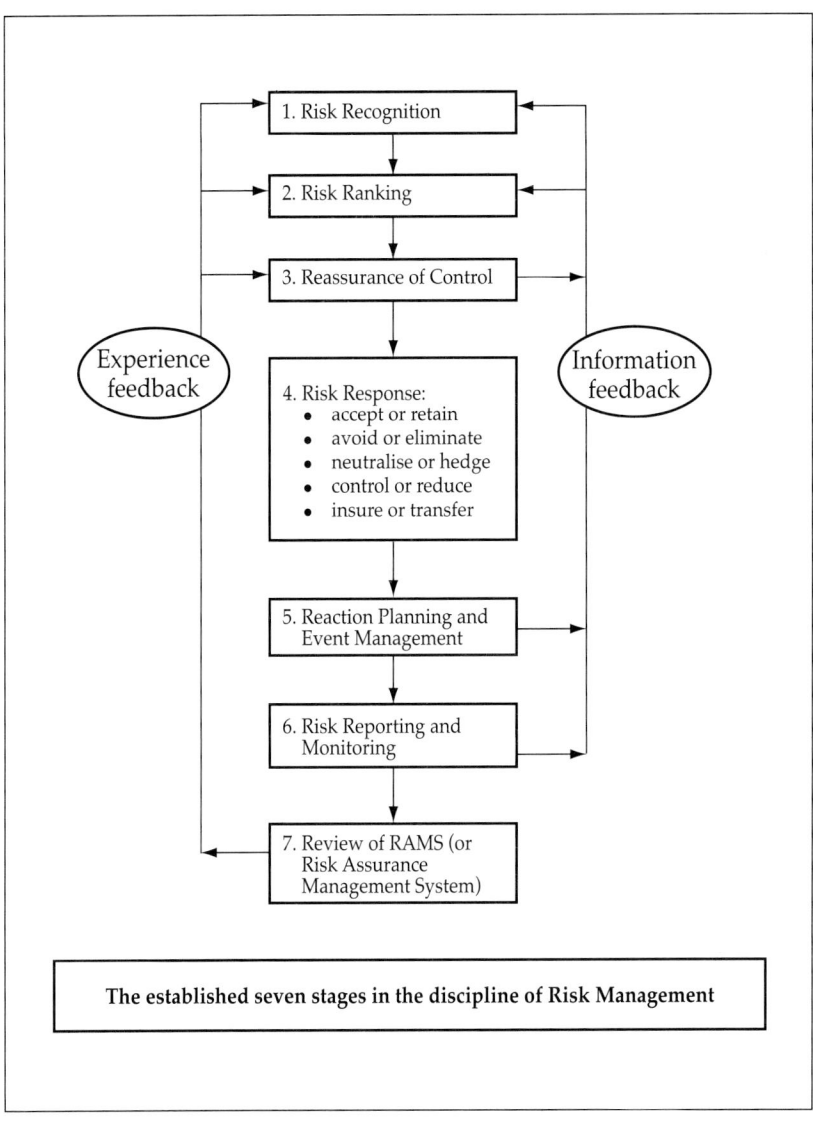

Figure 2: Risk Management Discipline

4. **Response to Significant Risks,** including decisions on the appropriate action regarding the following:

   - risk acceptance or retention
   - risk avoidance or elimination

- risk neutralisation or hedging

- risk control or reduction

- insurance or risk transfer

5. **Reaction Planning** and/or Event Management. For hazard risks, this may be described as disaster, recovery or business continuity planning.

6. **Reporting and Monitoring** of risk performance, actions and events and communicating on risk issues, via the risk architecture for the organisation.

7. **Review of Risk Assurance Management System (RAMS),** including internal audit procedures and arrangements for the review and updating of the risk architecture, strategy and protocols.

Each of these seven stages is described in more detail in the sections that follow. An important point to note is that the discipline of risk management must be dynamic and forward looking, this is why the phrase integrative risk management is preferred to the use of integrated risk management. The discipline must be applied in a way that is creative and must not be based on protocols that the risk manager has created. It is also worth emphasising that risk management is not only about hazard management. The tools and techniques (and the stages in the risk management discipline) are equally applicable to control risks and opportunity risks, as well as hazard risks.

2.1.1   Recognition of Risks

Recognition or identification of risks is the first stage of the risk management discipline. There are various techniques available for the identification of risks. Separate exercises to identify hazard risks, control risks and opportunity risks may be necessary, but there are advantages in identifying all risks first and then deciding on the nature of each risk (or CASE) afterwards.

Asking each of the following questions of each key dependency would facilitate these separate hazard, control and opportunity exercises:

- what could go wrong (hazard risks);

- what needs to be controlled (control risks); and

- what must go right (opportunity risks)

Risk identification will be a relatively easy activity for the organisation, assuming that the appropriate staff and managers are involved. Most risks are well known to people who work within the organisation. The main benefit of a formal risk identification exercise is that a common language and understanding of risk will be established and agreed. Staff and other people who work in or with the organisation will have a very good idea of what can go wrong, what causes uncertainty and what could make things better.

Although the risks will be well known within the organisation, the problem of structuring the risk identification exercise needs to be addressed. There is a danger that too many, apparently unrelated, risks will be identified. This will create the situation often referred to as "risk overload". The use of a risk matrix will be of assistance when recording details of the risks that have been identified. The idea of a risk matrix is discussed in more detail in Chapter 9.

The risk identification stage needs to be comprehensive and well structured. Evaluation of risks in relation to the mission, corporate objectives, stakeholder expectations and the core processes will be necessary. The significance of each risk must be evaluated in relation to the key dependency that would be impacted by the risk. Risks need to be identified in relation to each of the dependencies that support the core processes. The outcome of the risk identification stage will be a list (or matrix) of the potentially significant risks that could impact the key dependencies, core processes, stakeholder expectations, corporate objectives and the corporate mission.

A benchmark test for significance will need to be applied at each step in the risk identification exercise. Taking into account the local circumstances within which the risk arises. A risk may be significant for a department, but not for the organisation overall. Such a risk would appear in the departmental risk register but not in the corporate risk register.

2.1.2   Ranking of Risks

Ranking or evaluation of each of the identified risks needs to be undertaken in order to identify those risks that are significant. Each risk needs to be ranked in terms of the magnitude of the impact of the risk and the likelihood of the risk materialising at or above the benchmark level set as the test of significance. The aim of the risk ranking stage is to assist with completion of the risk assessment activity for the organisation. The importance of this stage of the risk management discipline is that it will ensure that the organisation focuses on the significant risks it faces, rather than using resources to manage less important CASE. Agreement on the priority risks facing the organisation is also part of avoiding risk overload.

The distinction between hazard risks, control risks and opportunity risks is important when producing the risk profile of the organisation. In the past, the phrase risk profile has been used to refer to hazard risks only. However, the questions below are equally applicable to hazard risks, control risks and opportunity risks:

- what could happen (or what is the CASE)

- could it impact above the benchmark level for significance

- how likely is it to happen at or above the benchmark level

The order in which the questions magnitude and likelihood are asked is important. The first stage of the identification of the priority significant risks is to decide what level of impact would be significant for the organisation. The question can then be asked whether a particular risk could impact at or above that level. If the risk is capable of such an impact, then the likelihood of the risk materialising at or above that level can be determined.

Some organisations will need to use more sophisticated risk ranking techniques because of the nature of the organisation. For example, petrochemical companies will need to establish the magnitude of an incident that would be significant and, then determine the likelihood, of such an incident (e.g. major fire or explosion) in quantified mathematical terms.

2.1.3 Reassurance of Control

Having ranked risks in terms of magnitude and likelihood, the next stage in the risk management discipline is to review the current status with respect to the management of these risks. For hazard risks, provision of appropriate resilience or duplication in buildings and services may be an important part of providing reassurance that the risk is under adequate control.

Each of the identified risks will have an inherent value that represents the magnitude and likelihood of the impact of the risk, in the absence of any controls. If a risk is potentially significant, the organisation is likely to have controls in place that reduce the inherent value to the current level. The reassurance of control stage in the risk management discipline assesses the acceptability of the current level and determines whether there is scope for further, cost effective, risk improvement.

Reassurance of control will be achieved when the current level of an individual risk is acceptable, however, a substantial amount of management resource may be used to achieve the state where the current risk level is satisfactory. The corporate resources utilised in moving from the inherent risk level to the current risk level is considered later in the book, both in relation to individual risks and the total corporate resources allocated to risk control.

There needs to be an appropriate level of confidence in the existing controls including a belief that the controls are practical and effective. This level of confidence can be recorded as a score related to the scope for further improvement in control. Clearly, if the scope for further improvement is high or very high, the level of confidence will be low. In these circumstances it is likely that there will be further actions that the organisation can reasonably take, or will feel obliged to take, in order to further improve control of the risk.

The joint stages of risk recognition, risk rating and reassurance of control are often referred to as "Risk Assessment". Risk assessment is the first recognisable and usable output of applying the risk management discipline. The result of the risk assessment will be the risk profile for the organisation and/or the register of significant risks. The risk register will identify and describe the priority significant risks and these risks will be subject to application of the later stages of the risk management discipline.

Note that a robust risk assessment is also the starting point for any effective system of internal control. It is worth noting that when a risk has existed in the organisation for some time, it may be described as being "mature". It is likely that the organisation will only undertake stages 1, 2 and 3 for such risks, because all mature risks would be expected to be adequately controlled.

2.1.4 Response to Significant Risks

The main reasons for undertaking a risk assessment are to:

- confirm that mature risks remain under adequate control;

- identify and evaluate the known significant risks; and

- analyse new and emerging risks

Further actions can be taken, as necessary, to ensure adequate management of the priority significant risks. Remember that a risk is significant if it could impact above the benchmark level for significance for that type of risk and thereby threaten the key dependencies that support the core processes that ensure the future existence of the organisation in its present size and form.

Following the recognition of the significant risks during the risk assessment exercise, it is necessary to respond to them. There are a wide range of responses available for the identified priority significant risks. Risk management effort needs to be focused specifically, but not exclusively, on the significant risks. The possible responses to these risks include:

- accept or retain

- avoid or eliminate

- neutralise or hedge

- control or reduce

- insure or transfer

The difference between the inherent and the current risk level is a measure of the corporate resources, in terms of time, money and effort, devoted to the management of that risk. The concepts of inherent and current risk levels can most easily be applied to hazard risks, although similar concepts can be defined for control risks and opportunity risks. It is worth considering the nature of inherent and current risk in more detail at this stage:

- **Inherent Risk** is the value of the risk before any controls are applied by the organisation. If there is a high inherent risk, the risk is potentially significant. Controls will need to be applied before the risk is considered to be under adequate control. Risks with a high inherent level will require greater management effort to ensure that the risk control standards are implemented.

- **Current Risk** is the value of the risk that exists, taking into account the controls already in place. This should be compared with any previous current level and with the inherent risk level. The greater the difference between the current risk and the inherent risk, then the more effort and resources the organisation is putting into controlling that risk and, the lower will be the scope for further cost effective risk improvement.

Corporate resources are used when risks are managed and the response to any risk needs to be proportionate to the impact that the risk could have on the core processes of the organisation. The generally accepted options for managing risks, especially in relation to hazard risks, are considered in more detail below:

- **accept or retain** – If the risk current level is acceptable then the organisation may decide to retain the risk. This will be the case when the level of current risk is acceptable in relation to the corporate resources allocated to the management of that risk. Although risk levels may be high, an organisation may decide to stay in a high risk segment of the market because it is potentially profitable and/or such processes are fundamental to the nature of the organisation.

- **avoid or eliminate** – Risk elimination is another option for the organisation. It may be that the risks of trading in a certain part of world or the environmental risks associated with continuing to use certain chemicals are unacceptable to the organisation, and/or its stakeholders. In these circumstances appropriate responses would be: elimination of the risk by stopping the process or activity, substituting an alternative process or outsourcing the activity.

- **neutralise or hedge** – Sometimes risks are only accepted as part of an arrangement whereby one risk is balanced against another. This is a simple description of neutralising or hedging risks, however, on a business level this may represent a fundamentally important strategic decision. An electricity company operating in the northern states of the USA may have to accept the impact of variation in temperature on electricity sales. By merging, or setting up a joint venture, with an electricity company in the southern states, the north/south combined operation will be able to smooth the temperature related variation in electricity sales.

- **control or reduce** – Actions to improve the standard of risk control will always be under constant review in an organisation. To use everyday examples, wearing a seatbelt when driving a car or fitting a car with an immobiliser are risk reduction actions. Improvements to standards of risk control in relation to physical or insurable risks are well known. Fitting sprinklers to buildings, providing enhanced building security arrangements and employee security vetting are all examples of risk improvement actions designed to better manage hazard risks.

- **insure or transfer** – Insurance is a well established mechanism for transferring the financial consequences of losses arising from hazard risks and, to a lesser extent, control risks. In some cases risk transfer is closely related to risk elimination. Many risks however cannot be transferred to the insurance market; either because of prohibitively high insurance premiums or because the risks under consideration have, traditionally, not been insurable. Apart from insurance, another example of transferring risks is by contractual agreement between the parties involved.

2.1.5 Reaction Planning

When a risk materialises the organisation should have plans in place to respond. Reaction plans will include disaster plans, recovery plans and/or business continuity plans for hazard risks. Audit response plans can be put in place for control risks and event management plans are required for CASE that can be used to the benefit of the organisation (opportunity risks). (e.g. an organisation launching a new product should have plans in place to cope with an unexpectedly high level of demand.)

Damage limitation and cost containment are elements of the overall recovery planning process for hazard risks. The main elements of recovery planning are the development, rehearsal and, when necessary, implementation of plans to ensure continuity of core processes in the aftermath of a disruptive event. It remains the case that business continuity plans (BCPs) are most commonly produced in relation to events that could result from the loss, damage, or denial of access to physical assets.

There have been many high profile examples of the benefits of such recovery plans. Terrorist attacks in commercial areas can result in huge damage to property to the extent that buildings have to be vacated and company processes relocated. Organisations with well established and fully rehearsed BCPs have been able to gain significant positive publicity by demonstrating to customers the rigor of their management procedures.

2.1.6   Reporting and Monitoring

Organisations need to ensure that the means of reporting and communicating on risk issues are fully established. The communication arrangements will be part of the risk protocols for the organisation. These protocols will include details of the risk reports that are required, including information on the CASE that should be reported to head office. Reporting, monitoring and communicating on risk issues will be part of the risk architecture for the organisation. For some large organisations, a formalised risk management policy with supporting risk guidelines will be necessary. Suggested contents for such a policy and the risk guidelines are discussed in chapter 7.

The risk based measurements of performance or risk based key performance indicators (KPIs) should be labelled as risk productivity indicators (RPIs). Monitoring of the RPIs will become a fundamentally important part of the risk reporting and monitoring arrangements. It will be the responsibility of managers to monitor the RPIs, as well as having responsibility for other aspects of risk communication.

2.1.7   Review of Risk Assurance Management System

The review stage of the risk management discipline is more formal than the monitoring stage, although the two stages are related. Together these stages provide assurance that risks are being successfully managed within a robust framework. The review of risk performance may be integrated into a broader management review of the core processes. In that case, the review of risk performance will have been fully embedded into routine reports of the performance of the core processes within the organisation. This is a good arrangement because it means that the review, and the management, of risks is not separated from the context that gave rise to the risks. In these circumstances risk performance review may not be a seen as a stage of the risk management discipline, but rather an embedded part of normal, routine activities.

Reviewing the risk architecture, strategy and protocols (RASP) is a necessary part of evaluating the overall risk performance of the organisation. The review of risk performance should also extend to a periodic audit of the whole risk assurance management system (RAMS). This will enable the board of the organisation to report formally to stakeholders on risk issues, probably via the risk management committee and audit committee. Review of risk performance will also need to include consideration of whether the existing RPIs have been correctly selected.

The formal reports will need to be scrutinised by internal auditors, external auditors and finally by the audit committee. These reports can then form part of the internal control section of the annual report and accounts for the organisation. These requirements are obligatory for companies listed on the London Stock Exchange, as set out in the Turnbull Report published in 1999.

2.2.   Expectations of Risk Management

Risk management is a high profile management initiative that must deliver the benefits that have been promised. As risk management develops and becomes more sophisticated, there are increasing expectations of the discipline. Risk management practitioners have claimed that the discipline will reduce business uncertainty, assist share price protection and facilitate enhanced corporate governance.

In short, there is an increasing expectation that risk management will enable organisations to achieve more successfully, the corporate mission. Risk management is expected to make a positive contribution to the well being of an organisation and enhance the level of corporate governance. As with any other initiative, the purpose of undertaking a risk management initiative must be to achieve a sustainable step change in corporate performance.

Historically, the most common expectation of risk management is that it would make a contribution to reducing costs and reducing unplanned dysfunctional operation within the organisation. The desired state for any organisation is that of no unplanned dysfunctional events or NUDE. Internal auditors have practiced an alternative style of risk management in relation to control risks. The expectation previously placed on internal auditors was that a cost effective system of internal financial control be achieved.

Table 2 presents an overview of the seven stages in the risk management discipline and lists the specific activities that form part of the discipline. The outcomes associated with the specific activities are also listed. It is these outcomes that have to deliver the promised benefits. Risk management must additionally deliver opportunity management to the organisation. The expectations of the organisation have grown and the discipline of risk management needs to ensure that these expectations are realistic, relevant and, above all, met.

RM Stage	RM Activity	Risk Management Outputs
1. Recognition 2. Ranking 3. Reassurance	1. Risk Assessment	• Identification of Significant Risks • Risk Profile for Organisation • Register of Significant Risks
4. Response	2. Risk Control	• Risk Improvement Actions • Risk Control Standards • Risk Protocols and Procedures
	3. Risk Resourcing (including Insurance)	• Financial Planning and Protection • Allocation of Corporate Resources • Risk Strategy for Organisation
5. Reaction Planning	4. Event Management	• Cost Control and Containment • NUDE planned and achieved • Risk Impact Optimisation
6. Reporting 7. Review	5. Risk Assurance	• Risk Architecture for Organisation • Risk Productivity Indicators • Adequate Risk Control

The activities and outputs associated with Risk Management

Table 2: Risk Management Activities and Outputs

2.2.1 Risk Management Activities

The seven stages of the risk management discipline are delivered by undertaking five discreet activities. The outputs from these five risk management activities must improve overall business performance, if they are to add value to the management of the organisation. These activities are as follows:

1. Risk Assessment

2. Risk Control

3. Risk Resourcing

4. Event Management

5. Risk Assurance

Consider each of the five risk management activities (and the associated outputs) in more detail. The comments below relate mainly to hazard risks, but similar approaches to control risks and opportunity risks are also valid.

1. **Risk Assessment** leads to the identification of significant risks, so that the risk profile of the organisation is defined and the register of the priority significant risks can be produced. The success of a risk management initiative is fundamentally dependent on the accurate identification of the priority significant risks. These will be hazard, control and/or opportunity in nature. The outputs from the risk assessment bring into focus all of the risk management activities that follow.

2. **Risk Control** leads to risk improvement actions, establishment of risk control standards, risk protocols and procedures. The controls that are put in place may typically be physical controls for hazard risks, systems and procedures for control risks or market research and new business strategy evaluations for opportunity risks. In all cases the identification and allocation of appropriate risk productivity indicators (RPIs) is necessary. These are the measurements that will be used to monitor risk performance.

3. **Risk Resourcing** leads to financial planning and protection, allocation of corporate resources and the development of a robust risk strategy for the organisation. The organisation will need to ensure cost effective control of risks, so that only the necessary resources are allocated. Remember that the allocation of resources

to the management of risks utilises some of the risk capacity of the organisation. Allocation of resources should be validated in relation to the values at risk, the total risk exposure, as well as, the risk capacity of the organisation.

4. **Event Management** leads to cost control and cost containment, planning for and achievement of the state of NUDE and the optimisation of risk impact. For projects, event management is vitally important. The project team will need to ensure that they have analysed the priority significant CASE and made appropriate plans. Opportunity management also depends on event management, although the emphasis will be somewhat different. Plans should be made to cope with positive events, such as a sudden and unexpected increase in consumer demand, or the demise of a competitor.

5. **Risk Assurance** leads to the establishment of risk protocols for the organisation, the establishment of appropriate risk productivity indicators (RPIs) and confirmation of the achievement of adequate standards of risk control. Risk assurance is the combination of risk monitoring and the review of the risk management arrangements in the organisation. The importance of risk monitoring is recognised and much of this book is concerned with risk monitoring methods and approaches that embed risk management into routine management activities. Review of the risk management arrangements involves a more formalised audit of the risk assurance management system (RAMS) operating within the organisation.

2.2.2   Risk Management Outputs

It is the outputs from the various risk management stages and activities that are useful. The risk productivity approach is largely focused on the outputs from the risk assessment and the risk assurance activities. The production of the register of priority significant risks and the introduction of risk productivity indicators (RPIs) are the key components of the approach. The outputs from the activities of risk control, risk resourcing and event management are well understood in relation to hazard risks. There is, however, a need to ensure that the outputs from these well established activities are extended to include control risks and opportunity risks.

The appropriate person must own the outputs from the various risk management activities, as well as being the owner of the risk itself. The appropriate person will usually be the person who manages the key dependency that can be impacted by the risk. That manager is likely to report to the senior manager or director, who has overall responsibility for the core process that is supported by that key dependency.

One of the big challenges for risk management is to align risk management activities with core processes within the organisation. This will ensure that risk management becomes a dynamic and pro-active support to core business processes, rather than a separate, static set of activities undertaken by specialists.

2.2.3 Risk Management Professionals

There are many professionals in large organisations with an understanding of risk and a contribution to make to the management of the risks faced by the organisation. Unfortunately, there is seldom a common language of risk and there is often a lack of understanding of, and agreement on, the risks that should be treated as the priority significant. Risk management professionals need to work together to maximise the benefits to the organisation. The risk management professionals involved will include the following individuals, at least:

- Insurance Risk Manager

- Corporate Treasurer

- Finance Director

- Internal Auditor

- Compliance Manager

- Health, Safety and Environment Manager

- Business Continuity Manager

Externally, insurance brokers, insurance companies, accountancy firms and external auditors will also have a contribution to make to the improved management of risk in their client organisations. It is important that risk management professionals work together and make the appropriate contribution to risk management activities. It is also important that the benefits of the risk management discipline are embedded into the core processes within the organisation.

Risk management professionals must support the owners of the key dependencies, priority significant risks and the owners of the core processes, in a way that does not take away any line management responsibilities. Chapter 8 discusses the suggested and renewed role of the risk manager in more detail. In summary, the emerging role that is suggested for the risk manager is that of guardian of the risk architecture, strategy and protocols (GRASP).

The overall aim of risk management practitioners is to help with the creation, implementation and review of a risk assurance management system (RAMS). The custodian of the RAMS will need to be a board member as this will ensure that management of risks receives a sufficiently high profile. It will normally be that same board member who sponsors risk management discussions at the board and presents risk management reports to the board. Typically, the risk manager will report to that board member, in the new role for the risk manager of GRASP.

2.3.   Risk Productivity

Risk productivity is an important concept in as much as that it provides a focus for what integrative risk management can deliver and how it can be achieved. The approach is based on the view that the full risk capacity of the organisation must be utilised in a way that will result in risk management effort producing a positive return on the values put at risk by the organisation. It is important to differentiate between the actual risk exposure that the organisation faces and the desired risk capacity of the organisation, as sanctioned and agreed by the board.

Risk productivity is the concept that defines the contribution that can be made by risk management to the achievement of the mission of the organisation. The organisation should ensure that an appropriate risk to reward ratio is achieved on the risk exposure of the organisation. All organisations should be calculating the sums currently put at risk by the organisation, so that the actual risk exposure can be determined. The correlation between these risks can be evaluated to ensure accurate calculation of the adjusted risk exposure, as discussed in chapter 1. Appropriate risks can then be taken up to the risk capacity of the organisation. Steps need to be taken to measure the benefits of taking risk by the allocation of appropriate risk productivity indicators (RPIs).

The risk productivity approach sets out the means by which the organisation can achieve the level of sophistication that will work in that organisation. Risk productivity will also ensure that the organisation uses its full risk capacity, as discussed in chapter 5. In order to achieve risk productivity, the organisation needs to find methodologies to determine its risk capacity, calculate its current risk exposure and then decide how much of the risk capacity is to be allocated to the various priority significant risks. Empirical methods of calculating risk exposure and risk capacity are outlined in this book. Chapters 5, 6 and 9 provide the outline of the approaches that are suggested. Appendix B sets out a consolidated case study using the ideas offered throughout the book. The twelve steps to achieving risk productivity are summarised in Figure 9 in Chapter 9.

Summary and Review of Chapter 2

Section 1 sets out some of the basic issues for consideration in relation to the nature of the risk management discipline. There are seven clearly defined and inter-dependent stages involved in the risk management discipline. It is not a stand alone discipline and it should be combined with other management activities and responsibilities.

It is important that the benefits of a rigorously implemented risk management approach are understood and achieved. In fact, many organisations find that the risk assessment workshop held at the beginning of the risk management initiative provides immediate benefits as a means of focusing on risk issues. These benefits arise from the fact that detailed discussions are held with colleagues on risk issues in a structured way which may not have taken place previously within the organisation.

Section 2 examines the application of the risk management stages in terms of the activities, the outputs and the professionals who can make a substantial contribution. It is suggested that a major contribution to the management of the organisation will be achieved by the provision of support to the owners of core processes, key dependencies and significant risks to assist with the fulfilment of their risk management obligations and responsibilities.

All parts of the organisation and all risk management professionals need to make the contribution that is required. The approach will then become holistic and integrative. The end result will be embedded and fully aligned risk management activities.

The main message from this chapter is that risk management improves the management of the core processes of the organisation by optimising the outcomes from CASE. The stages, activities and outputs from risk management, as well as the professionals involved in these aspects of the discipline are inter-dependent components of the integrative whole. Case Study 2 (overleaf) consolidates the key messages outlined in this chapter.

Case Study 2: Theatre – (Part 1)

The case study concerns the Aldgate Theatre, an established provincial theatre that runs small productions, typically for between 2 and 4 weeks. The audience expects the performance on the night to be entertaining, very professional and to an excellent standard. They also expect the performance to be free from disruption.

The risk manager must be able to demonstrate that the risk management activities and outputs have improved the management of the core process "deliver the performance on the night". This case study looks at hazard risks in particular, although the priority significant control risks and opportunity risks that could impact this core process are also listed below.

There are many CASE that can impact the key dependencies that are vital to the successful delivery of any performance at the Aldgate Theatre. The risk assessment will lead to the identification of the priority significant risks. The list of priority significant risks is likely to include the following:

Hazard:	power cut
	absence of an actor
Control:	audience behaviour
	reaction of the critics
Opportunity:	quality of the technical staff
	profile of actors in the cast

Risk control standards will be set to reduce the chances of a hazard risk materialising on the night. Business continuity plans will be in place to ensure that there will be a planned response to any disruptive event on the night. The arrangements may include, amongst others, fire drills, electrical generator back-up. Finally, the risk assurance arrangements will provide for review of the hazard risk performance, as well as review details of the mechanisms for the identification of any necessary risk improvements.

The outputs from the risk management discipline ensure that the core process "deliver the performance on the night" is more robustly managed than would otherwise have been the case. Risk management improves the management of this core process by optimising the outcome of any CASE that might materialise on the night.

Part 2

RISK MANAGEMENT IN CONTEXT

3 Styles of Risk Management

Risk Management will bring benefits at whichever level of sophistication the organisation implements the discipline

This chapter describes the different styles of risk management that are currently practiced. More professions and disciplines are now involved in risk management than in previous years. This adds diversity to the development of the risk management discipline. Although they are closely related, there are three styles of risk management. These are:

1. Hazard Management;

2. Control Management; and

3. Opportunity Management

These three styles can be represented as a developing awareness of risk management within an organisation. At first an organisation may be aware of a new risk and the need to take appropriate action. This will lead to a need for the organisation to **Reform** in response to the hazard risk. As the organisation responds to the risk, it will seek to **Conform** with the appropriate risk control standards. As a result of this the organisation may realise that there are benefits to be obtained from the risk. The organisation will then have the ability to **Perform** and treat the risk as an opportunity risk.

The stages of Reform to Conform to Perform represent levels of sophistication. It is not always necessary for a risk to progress from hazard to control to opportunity, in some circumstances risks can regress. At any one time, a particular risk will be of a specific type in an organisation. Benefits can be obtained from the successful management of that risk at whichever level of sophistication is appropriate at the time. In summary, risk management need only be as sophisticated as the organisation requires in order to bring benefits.

3.1. Styles of Risk Management Explained

It is now widely recognised that there are 3 complementary styles of risk management. These styles are related to the nature of the risk under consideration. Hazard management, control management and opportunity management define and describe the approach and, to some extent, the level of sophistication that is applied to the risk by an organisation at any one moment in time.

Hazard risks will always have a negative outcome associated with the risk. The maximum value at risk acceptable to the organisation is the hazard tolerance. Control risks will have a cost associated with controlling the risks and this cost is the control acceptance. Opportunity risks have a range of possible outcomes from highly positive to highly negative. The intended and planned outcome is, of course, positive. The organisation will be willing to put resources at risk in pursuit of opportunity risks and this is the opportunity appetite of the organisation.

The hazard tolerance, control acceptance and opportunity appetite are the values that the organisation is willing to put at risk. The sum of these three components is the risk capacity of the organisation and represents the total value that the organisation wishes to have at risk. The total value at risk is the sum of the values at risk for the individual risks. The actual total value at risk may differ from the risk capacity. The risk exposure of the organisation needs to be adjusted to determine the extent to which the individual risks are correlated. If two risks are completed uncorrelated, then the organisation can accept both risks, whilst only counting the larger exposure when determining actual risk exposure. This calculation is done on the basis that both risks are unlikely to materialise in the period under consideration. Throughout the analyses in this book, a likelihood, or level of certainty, of 99% is used. That is, if the risk (or the pair of uncorrelated risks) is less likely than 1% to materialise, then it is ignored.

The risk productivity approach requires an organisation to calculate its risk capacity and then compare this with the adjusted risk exposure. Note that the value at risk, risk capacity and risk exposure all relate to inputs. Risk management tools and techniques are concerned with managing and optimising the outcomes of risks that materialise. In simple terms, risk management can make its most important contribution by ensuring that the organisation optimises the outcomes of events that occur.

The type of risk under consideration helps determine the style of risk management that will be applied. However, some risks may need to be managed using all three styles of risk management, at different stages in the lifecycle of the risk. In summary, the three styles of risk management can be viewed as follows:

- Hazard Management or the "Total Cost of Risk" approach of the insurance world   1980's

- Control Management based on the internal control approach of internal auditors   1990's

- Opportunity Management is the interface between risk management and strategic planning   2000's

The insurance risk manager will normally manage motor vehicle risks as a loss minimisation or "Total Cost of Risk" issue. The avoidance of internal fraud will normally be managed as an internal control issue and will be monitored and reviewed by the internal audit department. Risks associated with a merger or acquisition should be managed as an opportunity issue by the CEO or nominated senior executive.

Figure 3 represents the relationship between risk and uncertainty. It illustrates the typical range of outcomes for hazard risks, control risks and opportunity risks. By including all three types of risk in a single figure, it is possible to demonstrate that the three types of risk are related and inter-dependent. The sum of all of the hazard tolerances plus control acceptances plus opportunity appetites will represent the total risk exposure of the organisation. It is equivalent to the total value that the organisation has at risk. When the values at risk have been correctly allocated, the total risk exposure should be equal to the risk capacity of the organisation. If too much or too little has been allocated, then the organisation will fail to make full use of its risk capacity. The decisions on allocation of risk capacity need to pay full regard to the correlation between the risks, as discussed earlier.

Figure 3 deserves more detailed analysis, because it is the basis for distinguishing between the three styles of risk management. The horizontal axis represents value at risk and each risk will utilise part of the risk capacity of the organisation. It demonstrates hazard tolerance on the left hand side through control acceptance in the centre to opportunity appetite on the right hand side. The vertical axis illustrates the possible range of outcomes (99% certainty) when values are put at risk.

Note that as more value is put at risk, the greater will be the range of possible outcomes associated with the risk. For each value put at risk by a specific risk, there will be a range of possible outcomes. Figure 3 illustrates the range of outcomes from the "worst possible outcome (99%)" to the "best possible outcome (99%)". These lines are presented on the basis that the organisation wishes to plan its risk strategy and allocation of risk capacity to a 99% certainty.

A 99% certainty means that there is only a 1 in 100 chance that the outcome will be outside the lines. So, there is a 1 in 200 chance of the outcome being better than the best possible line and a 1 in 200 chance that the outcome will be worse than the worst possible line. The organisation is willing to accept a 1 in 200 chance of an unexpectedly large adverse outcome as a planning criterion. For planning and evaluation purposes, there is the presumption that if an event is less likely than 1 in 100, then it is not going to happen.

Agreement on the risk capacity of the organisation will enable the organisation to define the limit of the corporate resources that can be put at risk. This aggregation of risk may allow the organisation to investigate the availability of aggregate financial protection for the fully consolidated portfolio of resources at risk. Aggregation into the portfolio will take account of the degree of correlation between the risks in the portfolio. This aggregate protection may be provided by way of insurance or another financing mechanism.

To illustrate the fact that the greater the value at risk, the greater the range of outcomes, consider the case of a transport company. The company may be willing to tolerate vehicle accident costs of up to £500,000 per annum. The actual outcome for this level of hazard tolerance, as shown in Figure 3, may be in the range £400,000 to £800,000. That is a range of 20% lower to 60% higher than the limit of tolerance. If it is willing to tolerate losses of up to £2.5 million then the actual outcome may be in the range £1.25 million to £5 million. That is a range of 50% lower to 100% higher than the limit of tolerance. This analysis justifies the comment that more value at risk equals more uncertainty about the outcome or "risk is uncertainty".

At the same time as the hazard, control and opportunity styles of risk management were developing, there has also been considerable development in other specialist areas of the discipline. Project, clinical, financial, credit and market types of risk management have all continued to develop during the 1990's. Project management is a form of control management that has become very well established and now makes a substantial contribution to the successful delivery of projects and enhancements. The interest in project risk management continues to increase and it is briefly considered in chapter 4.

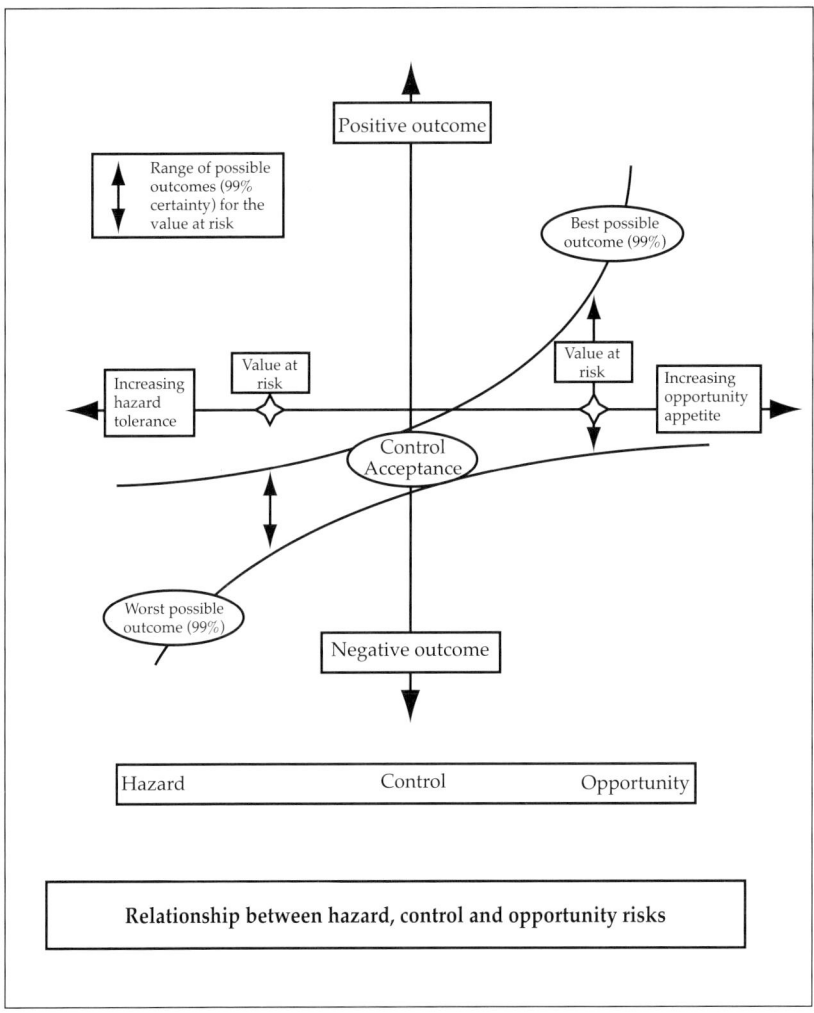

Figure 3: Risk and Uncertainty

3.1.1 Hazard Management

Hazard risks are the risks with the potential to inhibit, and only inhibit, the achievement of the corporate mission of the organisation. Hazard risks can also be considered to be threats or perils and these risks are likely to be insurable risks. Hazard management is the traditional approach adopted by the insurance world. Organisations can be considered to have a tolerance of hazard risks. The contribution that the insurance risk manager can make to hazard management is to reduce the likelihood and consequences of losses and thereby minimise the total cost of risk.

Figure 3 illustrates that, for hazard risks, the outcome will always be negative. There will be a range of possible outcomes and these are shown as a pair of 99% confidence lines. In all overall terms, the response to hazard risks will have the following three distinct phases:

1. Loss Avoidance   The actions taken in advance of the loss, to prevent the risk materialising

2. Damage Limitation   The actions taken at the time of the incident, to limit consequences

3. Cost Containment   The actions taken after the incident, to manage and/or reduce costs and disruption

Hazards will always have a negative outcome and so the valid approach is to minimise the downside. Hazard risks will always be evaluated in terms of criteria of failure and the benchmarks that are applied will always relate to things that the organisation would rather avoid. Hazard risks are associated with such words as tolerance, inhibit, failure and avoid. In Figure 3, the best possible outcome line will be improved by the application of risk control and loss management techniques and the worst possible outcome line may be limited by the use of insurance.

The caretaker of the Aldgate Theatre referred to in case studies 2 and 4 will be concerned with lighting failures and he will measure his performance in terms of how often the lights fail. This is a criterion of failure i.e. just because the lights do not fail,this does not mean that the audience will be satisfied with the lighting for the production. They will be evaluating the lights in terms of whether or not the lighting added to the enjoyment of the theatrical performance. This is a criterion of success.

The absence of criteria of failure for one stakeholder does not automatically mean the presence of criteria of success for another stakeholder. The caretaker will view lighting as a hazard risk that could cause dysfunction during the performance, but the audience will see it as an opportunity risk that should enhance their enjoyment of the performance.

3.1.2 Control Management

Control risks are the risks with potential to cause doubt or uncertainty about the achievement of the mission of the organisation. If the organisation removes or reduces the controls currently in place, there will be uncertainty about what will happen. This is the view of risk management adopted by auditors and accountants. The Turnbull report concentrated on internal control with very little reference to risk assessment. The internal control approach seeks to reduce the uncertainty associated with potentially significant risks.

There is a danger that the internal control approach to risk management could suppress entrepreneurial effort within the organisation. This is because control management is based on an aversion to doubt and uncertainty. Resources are allocated to the reduction of uncertainty, especially in relation to risks that are difficult to detect and measure, such as fraud. The control management approach seeks to reduce uncertainty associated with outcomes. It may drive an organisation to become less tolerant to hazards risks, but the approach may also result in a reduced appetite for opportunity risks. An approach based on enhanced internal control and the related reduction in uncertainty is a very restricted way forward for the discipline of risk management.

Control risks and control management are associated with such words as acceptance, doubt, uncertainty and minimise. When a risk level is shifted from the inherent risk level to the current risk level, corporate resources will be utilised. The use of some corporate resources to manage control risks is accepted as inevitable. The result is that part of the risk capacity of the organisation will be allocated to control acceptance. Although aspects of internal control will be familiar to the finance director, there may nevertheless be a reluctance to allocate more than the absolute minimum corporate resources to control acceptance.

In making a positive contribution to the organisation, internal control should move both lines upwards in Figure 3. As the lines are moved further upwards, then more risk capacity will be allocated, because the cost of internal control, as represented by the control acceptance, will be increased. Organisations should ensure that the control acceptance does not become so high that it consumes too much of the corporate risk capacity. The result will be that control risks become over-managed, to a point well past the stage of cost effective control.

3.1.3   Opportunity Management

Opportunity risks are the risks with potential to enhance (although they can also inhibit) the achievement of the corporate mission of the organisation. These risks are associated with taking advantage of business opportunities. Note that in extreme circumstances, an opportunity risk could become, or revert to, a control risk or even a hazard risk. Opportunity management is the approach that maximises the benefits of taking entrepreneurial risks. Organisations have an appetite for opportunity risks. There is, therefore, a close allegiance between opportunity management and strategic planning. The contribution that risk management can make in the area of opportunity management is to maximise the likelihood of a significant, positive outcome arising from taking entrepreneurial risks.

Most organisations already practise opportunity management although it may not be explicitly recognised as a risk management approach. Ideally, opportunity management should be embedded into the procedures for developing and implementing strategy and/or taking advantage of business opportunities. Some organisations do have explicit opportunity management procedures for the evaluation of new business prospects.

Again, the application of risk management tools and techniques should be firmly embedded within the opportunity management activities for the evaluation of new business opportunities. One of the fundamental contributions that opportunity management tools and techniques can make is to ensure that strategic plans are successfully developed and fully implemented. Techniques used to improve the range of possible outcomes shown in Figure 3 in respect of opportunity risks will be Joint Ventures (JVs), hedging techniques and reward enhancement, possibly by way of incentive and bonus arrangements. These incentive plans could extend beyond staff to suppliers, contractors and consultants.

Opportunity risks are associated with words such as appetite, enhance, success and achieve. Opportunity risks will be measured using criteria of success and these will typically be financial measures. These measurements will include the level of sales, positive marketing effort or positive product reviews in the relevant trade press. All of these measurements can be identified as risk based key performance indicators and these indicators should be labelled as risk productivity indicators or RPIs.

3.2. Risk Management Contribution

There are three styles of risk management based on the type of risk under consideration. A particular risk could be a hazard risk, control risk or opportunity risk in different organisations, or in the same organisation at different times. To gain maximum benefit from a risk, the organisation should, where possible, seek to shift the risk towards opportunity status.

Each style of risk management will make its own contribution to the management of a particular risk within the context that gave rise to that risk. Managing all risks in all situations as internal control issues will not offer the organisation the best contribution from risk management. Similarly, considering that all risks should be linked to insurance arrangements will lead to the situation where uninsurable risks are managed separately and differently from the more traditional, insurable, types of hazards risks.

In a rapidly developing discipline, like risk management, there is scope for the different practitioners to become intolerant towards the approach adopted by others. Internal control specialists who consider that risk management is associated with the management of uncertainty and the achievement of corporate objectives should not become intolerant of the more traditional insurance risk management approach. There is no value in one group of specialists being dismissive of the approach adopted by others or being unwilling to utilise the expertise that is available in another group.

There is no single style of risk management or approach to risk management that offers all the answers. Clearly, the various styles that can be adopted should operate as complementary approaches within an organisation. The integrative approach to risk management accepts that the organisation must tolerate certain hazard risks and must have an appropriate appetite for opportunity risks. Risk management tools and techniques should be brought to bear whereby the range of possible outcomes is shifted as follows:

- hazard management limits the negativity of the outcome
- control management reduces the range of outcomes
- opportunity management makes outcomes more positive

The recently published Turnbull Report is focused almost exclusively on internal control. There is little mention of risk assessment, there is no mention of opportunity risks or the benefits of opportunity management. Nevertheless, it is the Turnbull Report that is driving the risk management agenda at the moment. Organisations should not consider that Turnbull compliance represents the full contribution that can be made by risk management. Further advantages can be derived from opportunity management. In order to maximise the benefits, organisations need to decide the executive responsibility for co-ordinating opportunity management efforts. At present, this responsibility has not been allocated in most management structures.

3.2.1 Contribution of Hazard Management

Hazard Management will reduce the negative impact of any CASE that materialise. Within the context of hazard management, insurance represents the mechanism for restricting the financial cost of the losses, when a risk materialises. Given the nature of hazards, there is an expectation that hazard risks will have a negative outcome and there will be a financial cost to the organisation.

Risk control and loss management techniques will reduce any expected losses and should ensure that the overall cost is contained. The combination of insurance and risk control/loss management will reduce the actual cost of hazard losses and this will inevitably, and correctly, cause the hazard tolerance of the organisation to reduce. More of the risk capacity of the organisation will then be available for opportunity appetite.

If losses of £5 million can be tolerated, but the actual loss is £2 million, then the £3 million reduction in actual losses compared with the maximum hazard tolerance is not the upside of risk. Nevertheless, the fact that something did not go as wrong as expected is a positive outcome and the risk owners have clearly achieved a good standard of hazard management. However and very importantly, if losses of £5 million can be tolerated, but losses of £8 million occur with insurance paying the additional £3 million, that is certainly not to be seen as a profit from the insurance world.

3.2.2 Contribution of Control Management

Control management reduces the range of possible outcomes from any CASE. Control management is based on the established techniques of internal financial control, as practiced by internal auditors. The main intention is to reduce losses associated with inadequate control management at the same time as reducing the range of possible outcomes. This is the contribution that internal control should make to the overall approach to risk management within an organisation.

Although control management has a contribution to make to the organisation, there are disadvantages associated with this style of risk management. In particular, there is a danger that entrepreneurship will be suppressed in the organisation, because of the difficulty in gaining financial support for new ideas and opportunities. There is also a danger that known risks will become over-managed, well past the point of cost effective management of the risk.

3.2.3 Contribution of Opportunity Management

Opportunity Management seeks to make positive outcomes more likely and more substantial. Assume that an organisation is willing to spent £5 million on the development and launch of a new product with a two year life cycle. The business case for the new product predicts that sales during the 2 years will generate revenue of between £3 million and £15 million. In other words, it is anticipated that over the 2 years of the product life cycle, the result will be, with 99% certainty, in the range of a loss of £2 million and a profit of £10 million.

The organisation may decide that the £5 million opportunity appetite is acceptable, but that the total income must be at least £5 million. That is, the proposed new product must not make a net loss. The option of some kind of hedging may be considered, together with the possibility of a joint venture. These are the management options for reducing the potential downside. In effect, hedging and joint ventures will enable the organisation to put less value at risk and thereby reduce volatility of the profit or outcome.

As part of the opportunity management approach, the organisation should also look at possibilities for increasing the revenue from the product. These reward enhancement options can be discussed at strategy meetings and some options may be adopted, including the introduction of bonus and incentive schemes. If the decision is taken to pursue any of these options then risk productivity indicators (RPIs) should be attached to the selected actions, so that progress can be tracked.

The overall intention of opportunity management is to assist with the shift from a position where the organisation launches e.g:

- 20 new products per annum with

  ○ 11 successes;

  ○ 6 neutral outcomes; and

  ○ 3 failures;

to a position where the organisation launches e.g:

- 17 new products per annum with

  ○ 12 successes;

  ○ 4 neutral outcomes; and

  ○ only 1 failure

More detailed assessment of which products are to be launched and a greater success rate associated with the number of products actually launched will be the beneficial outcomes.

3.3.   Reform to Conform to Perform

Figure 3 illustrates that the three types of risks faced by an organisation can be considered as a continuum. Figure 4 shows the relationship between the level of sophistication applied to a risk and the contribution that each of the three styles of risk management can make to the organisation. This analysis is based on the premise that risk is a single transferable commodity. Remember that organisations can allocate corporate resources to the following:

- reserves (or reserve funds);

- revenue (or routine expenditure); and

- risk (or risk exposure)

As levels of sophistication in risk management increase, then the benefits will be enhanced. The stages in increasing sophistication could move the organisation through the following levels, depending on the nature of the risk under consideration:

- awareness of non-compliance   –   **REFORM**

- actions to ensure compliance   –   **CONFORM**

- achievement of business opportunities   –   **PERFORM**

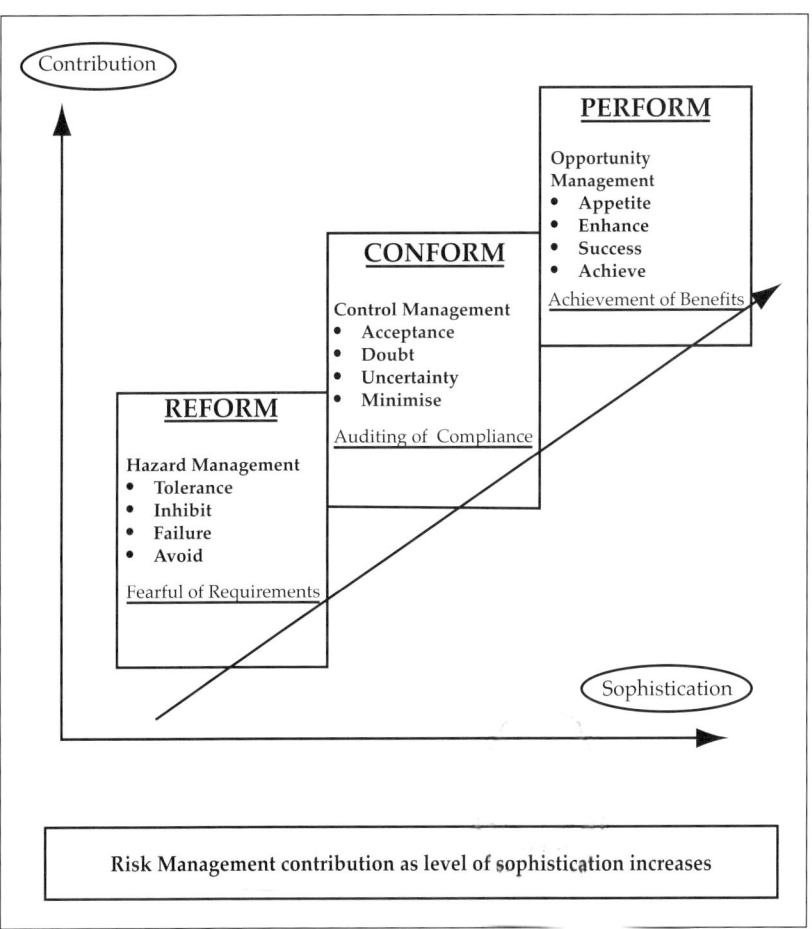

Figure 4: Risk Management Sophistication

Although the approaches of hazard management, control management and opportunity management represent three distinct styles of risk management, there is the potential for a risk to change and develop. In other words, hazard can become control can become opportunity. When this is achieved, the organisation will have moved from Reform to Conform to Perform.

As the level of sophistication increases and risk management professionals become aware of the alternative approaches to risk management, these professionals must start to value the contribution that each can make. In summary:

- hazard management specialists must accept that there may be a reduced desire to retain insurable risks (and buy more insurance) as a result of a more holistic approach to risk management;

- control management specialists must not squeeze entrepreneurial spirit and effort out of the organisation; and

- strategic planners must recognise that risk management tools and techniques can contribute to the successful exploitation of business opportunities.

Summary and Review of Chapter 3

Section 1 sets out the three different styles of risk management. All three styles will need to be applied in an organisation. It is worth noting that historically the different types of risks have been managed in different ways and this distinction continues to be valid, to some extent. In fact, the same risk will often have all three styles applied to it by the organisation during the life cycle of the risk, before it is finally retired, because it is no longer a priority significant risk.

It is important to recognise the full range of risk management approaches that can be applied, when appropriate. This will also help individuals and organisations to realise that risk management is a dynamic and developing discipline.

Section 2 examines the different levels of sophistication that can be applied and all levels will produce a positive contribution at any one time. It was suggested that additional benefits will be achieved as the level of risk management sophistication increases in the organisation.

At all levels of risk management sophistication, the organisation will be able to gain from what is currently a high profile management initiative. Alignment and embedding of risk management activities with operations, projects and strategy will ensure maximum benefits.

The main message from this chapter is that risk management need only be as sophisticated as the organisation requires for it to bring benefits. Reform to Conform to Perform is a very useful summary of what can be achieved. Case Study 3 consolidates the key messages outlined in this chapter.

Case Study 3: Magazine Publisher – (Part 1)

This case study concerns Barbican Publishing Limited. The company is based in London and produces a wide range of magazines for female readers, in the age range 12 to 18.

The senior management of the company became aware of the need to take action to fully comply with Equal Opportunities legislation about 3 years ago. The reaction was that the organisation needed to **Reform** in order to comply with this set of legal obligations. The position of not complying was seen as failure to manage a hazard risk. Barbican Publishing took the necessary actions to comply with the legislation and was pleased to reach the position of **Conform** after about 12 months.

Compliance with Equal Opportunities legislation was then seen as a control risk that required a certain amount of management time and effort to ensure continued compliance. There was an acceptance of a cost associated with compliance. The control acceptance cost was considered to be appropriate and necessary, but without commercial or financial benefit. There was also a feeling of doubt or uncertainty about what would happen if the controls were removed.

It then became clear to the senior management of Barbican that the organisation had a huge new asset. That asset was the section of the workforce from the minority ethic communities. The company planned a project to ensure that it would move to a position of **Perform**. That is, the publisher would be able to widen the appeal of its magazines by using the diversity in its workforce to publish articles, and eventually new titles, aimed at ethnic minorities. Barbican Publishing has now moved from Reform to Conform to Perform over the course of 3 years.

This is an example of an organisation becoming more sophisticated in its approach to risk management. Equal Opportunities and race discrimination developed from hazard risk to control risk to opportunity risk. Note that, at each stage, risk management was able to make a significant contribution. So, as this example conveys risk management need only be as sophisticated as the organisation requires, in order to make a worthwhile contribution.

4 Embedding Risk Management

Risk Management must be aligned with the mission of the organisation in order to achieve lasting benefits

This chapter considers the mechanisms for embedding risk management into the business cycle. A model of the business cycle is offered and the contribution that risk management tools and techniques can make is outlined. Ensuring that risk management is fully embedded is vitally important. This will ensure that the actions taken to improve management of risk are considered as part of the routine review of the core processes within the organisation.

Three types of core processes are outlined in this chapter. These are the core processes related to the:

- continuity and monitoring of routine operations;
- management of projects and enhancements; and
- development and delivery of strategy;

The options for embedding risk management into each of these types of core processes are considered.

Core processes define the business imperatives of the organisation. The core processes deliver the mission, corporate objectives and stakeholder expectations. Core processes are supported by key dependencies that can be impacted by risks. Risk management, therefore, has to be embedded within these core processes. Indeed, risk management must be fully aligned with the mission of the organisation to achieve lasting benefits. Because key dependencies are so vital, the approach to risk management that is "dependencies-driven" will be more thorough and successful than the alternative and more common "objectives-driven" approach.

4.1.   The Business Cycle

Risks must be managed within the context that gave rise to the risks. The context that gives rise to the risks can be defined and understood by reference to the business cycle. Figure 5 suggests a simple model of the business cycle that can be used as a framework for the description and understanding of risk productivity. It is worth reminding risk management specialists and enthusiasts that organisations do not exist for the primary purpose of managing risks, any more than they exist for the primary purpose of employing people. Risk management should be seen as a discipline that can facilitate a sustainable step change in the successful achievement of the corporate mission.

The main features of the business cycle can be described and considered under the following headings:

1.   Mission Statement

2.   External Evaluation

3.   Internal Evaluation

4.   Stakeholder Expectations

5.   Corporate Objectives

6.   Core Processes

A diagrammatic representation of the stages of the business cycle is set out in Figure 5 and discussed below. Stages 1, 2 and 3 are closely linked and there needs to be a feedback loop between these three stages. Every organisation should focus on the core processes of the organisation. It is the core processes that deliver the mission, corporate objectives and stakeholder expectations. The senior management structure of the organisation should reflect the need to manage the core processes that exist within the organisation.

There are three types of core processes, as described in earlier chapters. These core processes are supported by key dependencies and it is the key dependencies that can be impacted by risks. The approach advocated in this book is that of "dependencies-driven" risk management, rather than the "objectives-driven" risk management which is more usually recommended by consultancy firms. Responsibilities for key dependencies and/or the risks that could impact these dependencies should be defined within the management structure established to manage the core processes.

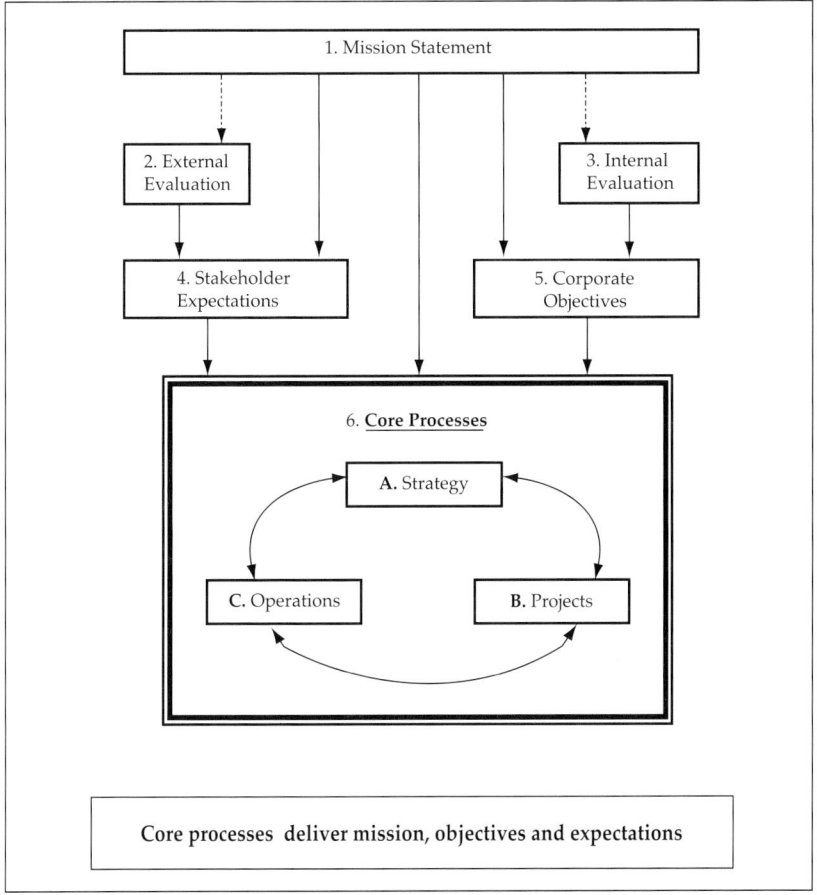

Figure 5: Model of the Business Cycle

4.1.1 Mission Statement

The corporate mission defines the fundamental aim of the organisation and it implies the reason for the existence of the organisation. Typically, the mission will be brief and not contain too much detail. An organisation may decide that the mission is "to help homeless people in London" or "to be the biggest supplier of bottled water in Britain".

The mission is a good place to start for risk management, because it represents an unambiguous statement of why the organisation exists. It implies what measurements or key performance indicators will be used to determine the ultimate success or effectiveness of the organisation. It is worth sounding a word of caution at this point. The mission statement may have become out of date or it may be too ill-defined or vague. An example of an ill-defined mission statement would be "to deliver shareholder value".

4.1.2 External Evaluation

The review of the internal and external aspects of an organisation can be undertaken by several techniques, including the well established strengths, weaknesses, opportunities and threats (SWOT) evaluation. Alternatively, a political, environmental, social and technological (PEST) analysis can be undertaken. These established brainstorming techniques are a useful way of structuring the collection of information.

Every organisation needs to know the business environment within which it exists. Many organisations will start the business cycle by looking at the external environment and identifying the opportunities that exist or are developing. All organisations will wish to rapidly respond to appropriate opportunities that come to its attention. Generally speaking, the external evaluation leads to the identification of the stakeholders and the stakeholder expectations.

The external evaluation will focus on the opportunities and threats in the marketplace and the opportunities and threats associated with the reputation of the organisation. This stage of the business cycle leads to the formulation of strategy. Risk management tools and techniques can assist with the formulation and implementation of that strategy.

4.1.3 Internal Evaluation

The internal evaluation can be undertaken using a strengths and weaknesses analysis for the whole organisation. However, an alternative approach is to identify the business opportunities in the external review phase and then undertake a separate strengths and weaknesses analysis for each viable opportunity, in turn. This opportunity by opportunity approach will only be fully successful if the organisation has not missed any of the relevant and valid opportunities in the external environment.

A strengths and weaknesses approach is an evaluation of what the organisation is capable of doing, this is the internal evaluation stage. This helps to define and, perhaps, limit the scope of opportunities that the organisation could realistically consider. Generally speaking, corporate objectives are produced as the output from the internal evaluation of the strengths and weaknesses of the organisation. It is clear that the internal evaluation and the external evaluation are interdependent and must be undertaken together.

Taken together, the internal and external evaluation stages should ensure that the:

- organisation takes best advantage of identified opportunities

- threats to fulfilling each opportunity are identified and managed

- internal strengths are used to maximum advantage

- internal weaknesses are reduced in their possible impact

4.1.4 Stakeholder Expectations

All organisations have stakeholders with an interest in the processes undertaken by the organisation. The stakeholders will be individuals, groups and/or other organisations. Many organisations will have stakeholders that they do not want, such as pressure groups or lobby groups. For example, chemical companies will have expectations placed on them by environmental pressure groups.

Some of the stakeholders will be internal to the organisation and the remainder will be external. The outcomes from the analysis of stakeholder expectations will complement the work leading to the identification of corporate objectives. This is beneficial, because it ensures that the approaches are complimentary and the overall exercise becomes more robust and complete.

For most organisations, the stakeholders will be compromised of the following:

- customers

- staff

- financiers and shareholders

- sponsors and suppliers

- pressure groups

- Government

Stakeholder expectations may be contradictory or even mutually exclusive in terms of the demands placed on the organisation. Also, unwanted stakeholders, will have, sometimes unreasonable, expectations that cannot be ignored. The identification of stakeholder expectations is part of the output from the external evaluation stage of the business cycle.

4.1.5   Corporate Objectives

Corporate objectives are identified during the internal evaluation and analysis of the mission statement. There is a danger that corporate objectives will be stated as internal, annual, change objectives. In order for "objectives-driven" risk management to be successful, it will be necessary to produce a full set of corporate objectives. When producing its objectives, an organisation must also focus on aspects of the routine processes within the organisation. This will facilitate the production of a full statement of the short term, medium term and long term objectives of the organisation.

A full statement of objectives should set out those objectives related to the following aspects of the current operations and future success of the organisation:

1.   Efficiency (or operational);

2.   Change (or competition); and

3.   Strategic (or market leadership)

These three aspects correspond to the three types of core processes that have already been described.

Note that corporate objectives could be set out using the framework of the FIRM Risk Scorecard that is described in chapter 5. Use of the FIRM Risk Scorecard facilitates the identification of objectives related to the financial, infrastructure, reputational and marketplace aspects of the future of the organisation. The setting of objectives is itself a core process of the "development and delivery of strategy" type.

Taking the existing objectives of the organisation as a starting point for risk management assumes that they are correct. The main danger with the so-called "objectives-driven" risk management approach is that it could be based on a poorly defined partial picture of the organisation, especially if the objectives are not correctly written. Objectives are a high level, conceptual view of the organisation and they may be too intangible for the attachment of risks.

4.1.6 Core Processes

A core process is fundamental to the continued success, or even existence, of the organisation in its present size and form. Core processes ensure that the organisation is able to achieve the mission, corporate objectives and stakeholder expectations. Each core process creates value in the organisation and is designed to deliver one or more of the stakeholder expectations.

There are three basic types of core process as set out in Figure 5. These are processes designed, implemented and managed to ensure the following:

A. Continuity and monitoring of routine operations

B. Management of projects and enhancements

C. Development and delivery of strategy

An activity is an individual job or task undertaken within the organisation. These activities build into the processes that deliver stakeholder expectations. Each additional activity within a process adds cost, but should make the process more robust and effective. The processes themselves are designed and intended to add value.

The case study in Appendix B gives actual examples of the different types of core processes. Processes concerned with continuity and monitoring of routine operations are designed to maintain efficiency. The risks to these processes are, in the main, hazard risks. Processes for the management of projects and enhancements ensure that the organisation keeps up with the competition and the risks in these processes are mainly control risks. Development and delivery of strategy processes relate to the provision and/or maintenance of market leadership. The risks associated with strategy core processes are usually opportunity risks.

Having identified the stakeholder expectations and determined the common expectations shared by stakeholders, core processes can then be put in place to ensure that these expectations are delivered to the level that the organisation has decided is appropriate. No organisation will be in a position to fully deliver all expectations to the level desired by all stakeholders. Weaknesses or gaps will be present, as follows:

- there may be weaknesses related to failure to ensure continuity and monitoring of routine operations. These weaknesses will result in the organisation failing to maintain efficient operations. These weaknesses give rise to an efficiency gap.

- there may be weaknesses related to the management of projects and enhancements. These weaknesses will result in the organisation failing to keep up with the competition. These weaknesses give rise to a competition gap.

- there may be weaknesses related to the development and delivery of strategy. These weaknesses will result in the organisation failing to retain its position as market leader. These weaknesses give rise to a leadership gap.

Measurement and monitoring are vitally important stages in the business cycle. The organisation needs to be aware of its performance and will select various key performance indicators (KPIs) that monitor the performance of core processes. Monitoring of performance should include evaluation of those risks that are the priority significant risks for the organisation. The KPIs attached to the priority significant risks should be designated as risk productivity indicators (RPIs). This will ensure that managers realise that these are risk based measurements. Awareness of the RPIs will enable the audit committee to monitor the contribution that risk management is making to the organisation and enable the audit committee to suggest areas for improvement.

For some organisations, it may be the case that separate procedures and systems to monitor risk performance may not be appropriate or necessary. It is much better for the organisation if risk performance is monitored by way of RPIs that are embedded into established process performance monitoring procedures. The role of internal auditors in these measurement processes should be carefully defined, so that their activities do not appear to take responsibility away from the owners of the risks.

Risk assurance is the combination of routine risk monitoring and the more structured risk review activities. Auditors will need to take an interest in all aspects of the risk assurance management system (RAMS) and will conduct some of the audit work directly. Apart from the routine monitoring of risk performance, auditors will also need to undertake a detailed review of the risk architecture, strategy and protocols (RASP), as well as the RAMS operating in the organisation.

The report of the review will be presented to the risk management committee, before being passed to the audit committee. It will finally be reported to the board for evaluation and approval. The board should also set strategy for the future management of risk within the organisation. As well as reviewing risk performance and RPIs, the review(s) will also consider and evaluate the current RASP of the organisation, the risk management policy and risk guidelines and compliance with Turnbull and other relevant obligations.

4.2.   Embedding Risk Management

Risk management needs to be embedded into the routine activities of the organisation. This will result in risk management activities taking place as part of the corporate diary of events in the organisation. Before this embedding of activities can take place, risk management needs to align the timetable of risk management activities with the timetable of other corporate events.

For example, consider the case of an organisation that requires the submission of the strategy plans from departments in May. In this case, the risk assessment activity should take place in April. The results of the profiling exercise can then act as an input into the production and validation of the strategy plan for each department, for submission in May.

The management of risk needs to be embedded into the management of the core processes. Decisions on whether a risk is potentially significant can only be taken with reference to the core process and key dependencies that would be impacted if the risk materialised. Apart from the exception mentioned below, only the priority significant risks need to be considered at boardroom level. This will ensure that the board focuses on the risks that are important to the future of the organisation.

The exception is that the board will also need to receive reports on compliance risks, so that it can be aware of legal requirements, request actions to be taken and receive re-assurance about the level of compliance achieved by the organisation. Compliance risks will include health and safety, environmental and equal opportunities risks.

4.2.1   Risk Management and Operations

Routine operations are fundamental to the continued existence of any organisation and these routine operations must be delivered efficiently. For routine operations, risk control is the most important of the five risk management activities. Risk control is fundamentally important to the successful and efficient management of these processes and the achievement of the desired state of No Unplanned Dysfunctional Events (NUDE).

The desired state of NUDE is more likely to be achieved if a hazard risk assessment is undertaken and risk improvement recommendations implemented. This will ensure that unplanned dysfunctional operation is kept to a minimum and it will also ensure that suitable business continuity and event management plans are in place should a risk materialise.

Routine operations are normally associated with hazard management, but aspects of control and opportunity management are also involved. As well as asking "what hazard risks could inhibit normal, efficient operation", the question "what opportunity risks could enhance normal efficient operation" should also be asked. It will often be the case that the opportunity risks identified in this way will simply be the opposite of the hazard risks. However, this will not always be the case and it is worth undertaking separate analyses, to ensure that the risk assessment is more comprehensive. Likewise, the question "what can cause doubt and uncertainty within an operational process" will enable the control risks to be identified and better managed.

Measurement and monitoring is fundamentally important and it delivers feedback on the performance of the core processes to confirm success. These monitoring processes are themselves routine operational processes. Risk productivity indicators (RPIs) are the risk based key performance indicators that will be used to ensure satisfactory risk performance within these operational core processes.

4.2.2 Risk Management and Projects

Project risk management is a type of control management. Projects relate to the delivery of a finite, specific or tactical issue such as:

- a building extension
- a new product launch
- a new IT system
- a new factory development
- exploiting new markets

Projects and enhancements are fundamentally important to the organisation. Most projects are undertaken either to keep ahead of competitors or to catch up with the competition. In the context of risk management, projects may be considered to be risk reduction exercises targeted at a specific management issue. The only purpose in spending money on projects is to achieve enhanced competitive advantage. It is fair to say, however, that this fact may not always be obvious to the department or business unit putting forward the project proposal.

The competition gap needs to be reduced so that the organisation may continue to be successful. When considering projects and project submissions, a hazard evaluation can be undertaken in order to answer the following question "what are the hazard risks that will stop us delivering the project within budget and on time?" Similar questions can be asked about the control risks and the opportunity risks. Project risk management is well developed, with risk control and (especially) event management being the risk management activities that are most important. Project risk management is one of the more sophisticated and successful areas of application of risk management tools and techniques.

The requirement for all projects is that they are delivered within the appropriate cost, time and quality parameters. Quality is the relationship between specification and performance. Projects must be delivered:

- within budget
- on time
- to specification
- to performance

Due to the nature of projects, historical loss data may not always be available. Accordingly, project risk management needs to be a forward looking discipline that anticipates problems. If available, historical experience of losses within similar projects may be useful. However, by the nature of projects, they tend to be one off activities without exact historical equivalent.

Hazard risks, control risks and opportunity risks need to be considered as part of the successful management of any project or enhancement. There are risks *to* the project (hazards), risks *in* the project (control risks) and risks *of* the project (opportunities). Projects should be viewed from the following three risk management perspectives:

- delivery of the project within budget and on time, this can be inhibited by hazard risks, or risks *to* the project;

- ability to deliver the project to specification and to performance relates to control risks, or risks *in* the project; and

- what the project is seeking to achieve is related to opportunity risks, or the risks *of* the project

4.2.3 Risk Management and Strategy

Strategy is fundamental to the continued success of an organisation. Successful development and delivery of strategy results in market leadership. Core processes concerned with development and delivery of strategy are highly dependent on robust risk assessment, as the most important risk management activity. Strategic core processes bring the disciplines of strategic planning and risk management together. The importance of the external review as part of strategy formulation has already been emphasised.

Strategic planning is a systematic process for obtaining a consensus at board level on the small number of issues that could have a massive effect on the long term performance of the organisation. It is worth remembering that stakeholder expectations will frequently relate to the long term performance of the organisation. An example of embedding risk assessment into strategic planning is to require that a copy of the outcome of the risk assessment, possibly in the form of a risk register, be attached to the strategic review plan for each department.

Strategic issues are vitally important and failure of strategy or the selection of an inappropriate strategy can be amongst the most devastating risks to hit an organisation. Strategy is a set of plans and actions to sustain economic value into the future. It will seek to exploit opportunities in the marketplace and will be the basis of long term economic value creation. Implementation of strategy is usually achieved by way of projects and then ultimately delivered by operational core processes.

4.3. Alignment of Risk Management

Risk management must be aligned with the mission and with the management timetables, or corporate calendar, within the organisation in order to achieve lasting benefits. Only when risk management is fully aligned with corporate activities can the benefits of risk productivity be achieved within the organisation.

Risk management needs to be aligned with many of the activities within the organisation. Mainly, it is about alignment of risk management with the routine or established procedures and protocols of the organisation. This will include ensuring that the scheduled risk management and internal control activities and meetings are included in corporate planning. These activities need to be compatible with and supportive of the corporate calendar.

Unless risk management activities are aligned with the key corporate dates in the organisation, there will be a danger that risk management will be seen as additional administrative burden and separate from the main task of successfully managing the organisation to achieve the corporate mission. Alignment will ensure that maximum benefits are achieved at optimal effort.

In order that maximum benefits are achieved risk management activities, in particular the preparation of routine risk assessments, will need to be aligned with other corporate activities. Risk assessments should be attached to at least the following:

- strategic plans
- project or capex submissions
- annual departmental budgets

These risk assessments should include consideration of the risks that can enhance, inhibit and cause doubt about the achievement of the plan, submission or budget. The exact nature of the risk assessment to be attached to any submission will depend on whether the relevant core process is an operational, project, or strategic one. Alignment of risk management activities is considered in more detail in chapter 9.

Summary and Review of Chapter 4

Section 1 identifies the expectations of stakeholders and the processes that deliver those expectations. Risk management tools and techniques can be firmly embedded into continuation of normal operations, the execution of projects and the formulation of strategy. However, the corporate objectives do not represent the best basis for identification of significant risks. These objectives may often be annual, internal, change objectives that are somewhat vague. In any case, corporate objectives are usually too intangible for the successful attachment of risks.

It is important to embed risk management into the protocols and procedures for the achievement of the mission. This will ensure that the key dependencies that support the core processes are carefully evaluated regarding the risks that can impact these key dependencies. Risk management considerations should be embedded into the operational budgets, project submissions and strategic plans.

Section 2 examines the need to embed risk management into operations, projects and strategy. It is suggested that the best chance of embedding risk management into corporate processes is to fully align the risk management activities with the timetable for reporting and other corporate diary events and activities.

The main message in this chapter is that risk management needs to be embedded into all aspects of the business cycle, including the development of the mission, evaluation of the internal and external environment and the development of corporate objectives. The other main message from this chapter is that risk management measurements by way of risk productivity indicators (RPIs) should be embedded into routine performance monitoring activities. Case Study 4 (overleaf) consolidates the key messages outlined in this chapter.

Case Study 4: Theatre – (Part 2)

The Aldgate Theatre is an established provincial theatre that runs small productions, typically for between 2 and 4 weeks. In case study 2, the contribution of risk management to the achievement of the "deliver the performance on the night" core processes was discussed. The mission of the Aldgate Theatre is "to become the leading presenter of low budget – popular entertainment productions in the country". Part 2 of the case study of the theatre concerns the "provide entertaining shows at low cost" core process.

To achieve this core process, the Aldgate Theatre often presents one man shows. An established actor is planning a one man show for a two week run at the Aldgate Theatre. He realises that a large proportion of the risks associated with his show are under his ownership and control. Accordingly, he may, when planning his one man show, set out the objectives that he is seeking to achieve. This would be sensible, but a broader view of what must be achieved is to analyse other stakeholder expectations. In particular, the expectations of the audience must be taken into account. Finally, the theatre management has expectations related to profitability, reputation, technical requirements etc.

If the actor plans his show only on the basis of his own objectives, he may fail to meet audience expectations, even though he has completely fulfilled his own objectives. The objectives of the actor will not be the same as the expectations of the audience. For example, an established musician may wish to promote the new album. Yet the audience will want to hear the established favourites from previous albums.

This is a clear example of the distinction between "objectives-driven" and "dependencies-driven" risk management. The actor will have the best chance of presenting a successful show if the starting point is an evaluation of the audience expectations, followed by an evaluation of the expectations of the Aldgate Theatre.

The author in turn can then plan the specific content of his show to be consistent with those expectations, as well as, very importantly, taking into account his own professional and personal objectives. After all, the actor is also a stakeholder himself, a very important stakeholder, but only one of the stakeholders.

Part 3

FIRM RISK SCORECARD

5 Classification of Risks

The FIRM Risk Scorecard ensures robust risk assessment and facilitates the allocation of risk capacity

This chapter considers the timescale for the impact of risks. Some risks have an immediate impact as soon as the CASE materialises and these are short term risks. Other risks have their impact some time after the CASE occurs. Typically, the delay will be months and these risks are medium term risks. Medium term risks are often the risks that attach to projects and enhancements. Other risks have their impact some considerable time after the CASE occurred and these risks are long term risks.

In order to identify all of the risks facing an organisation, a structure for risk identification is required. The FIRM Risk Scorecard provides such a structure. It builds on the different aspects of risk, including timescale of impact, nature of impact, whether the risk is hazard, control or opportunity and the overall risk exposure and risk capacity of the organisation. The headings of the FIRM Risk Scorecard provide for the further classification of risks as being primarily financial, infrastructure, reputational or marketplace in nature.

The FIRM Risk Scorecard can also be used as a template for the identification of corporate objectives, stakeholder expectations and most importantly, key dependencies. The FIRM Risk Scorecard is an important addition to the currently available risk management tools and techniques. The FIRM Risk Scorecard is compiled by analysing the way in which each risk could impact the key dependencies that support each core process. Use of the FIRM Risk Scorecard ensures robust risk assessment and facilitates the illustration of risk exposure and the allocation of risk capacity.

5.1 Short, Medium and Long Term Risks

Chapter 1 considered risks as hazard, control and opportunity. This is an important classification system, but it is not sufficient on its own as a means of identifying the nature of the risks faced by an organisation. Risks can have their impact at variable times after the circumstance, action, situation or event (CASE) occurs. Short term risks have an immediate impact, as soon as the CASE occurs. Other risks have their impact some months after the CASE and these can be labelled as medium term risks. Long term risks will have their impact some years after the CASE materialises.

The distinction between the different timescale of impact helps to identify risks as being related, primarily, to operational, project and strategic core processes. Although the distinction is not clear cut, it does assist with the further classification of risks. There will, in fact, be some short term risks to strategic core processes and there may be some medium term and long term risks that could impact operational core processes.

5.1.1 Short Term Risks

A short term risk has the ability to impact the key dependencies that support core processes with the impact being immediate. These risks can cause dysfunction immediately at the time the CASE occurs. Short term risks are predominantly hazard risks, although this is not always the situation. These risks are normally associated with unplanned dysfunctional events, but may also be associated with cost control in the organisation. Short term risks usually impact the ability of the organisation to maintain the core processes that are concerned with the continuity and monitoring of routine operations.

Short term risks are related to operations, but these risks should not be treated as being exclusively associated with hazard risks, hazard management and the management of operational type core processes. Short term risks should be viewed as CASE that can impact one or more of the key dependencies with the impact being immediate.

- an example of a short term risk would be the breakdown, hacking or virus infection of the computer system of the organisation. The CASE would be the hazard event and the consequences would be immediately known. The disruption or dysfunction would be apparent as soon as the adverse CASE occurred. The desired state of NUDE would not be achieved by the organisation.

5.1.2   Medium Term Risks

A medium term risk has the ability to impact the organisation a short time delay after the CASE occurs. Typically, the impact of a medium term risk would not be apparent immediately, but would be apparent within months, or at most a year after the CASE. Medium term risks usually impact the ability of the organisation to maintain core processes that are concerned with the management of projects and enhancements. These medium term risks are often associated with projects, tactics, enhancements, developments, product launch etc.

Medium term risks are related to projects, but these risks should not be treated as being exclusively associated with control risks, control management and the management of project type core processes. Medium term risks should be viewed as CASE that can impact one or more key dependencies, but the consequences of the impact will not materialise for some months, although probably within the current financial or planning/budgeting year.

- an example of a medium term risk would be the CASE related to the installation of a new computer system for the organisation. The CASE would be the risks in the project to upgrade the computer equipment. If the project is poorly managed, then the consequences may take some (fairly short) time to become known. The risks will be the actions and events associated with the installation of the new system, whereby the project fails to achieve the project plan.

5.1.3   Long Term Risks

A long term risk has the ability to impact the organisation some time after the CASE occurs. Typically, the impact could occur between 1 and 5 years, or more after the CASE. Long term risks usually impact the ability of the organisation to maintain the core processes that are concerned with the development and delivery of strategy.

Long term risks are related to strategy, but these risks should not be treated as being exclusively associated with opportunity risks, opportunity management and the management of strategic core processes. Long term risks should be viewed as CASE that can impact one or more of the key dependencies supporting the core processes, but the impact will not materialise for some (perhaps considerable) time.

- an example of a long term risk would be the selection of a new computer system for the organisation. The CASE would be the strategic decision to select a specific type of computer equipment. The decision is the event and ordering the new equipment is the action. If the decision is wrong, it will be some time before the consequences are known. Remember that the choice of new computer equipment will be taken as an opportunity risk that is intended to deliver significant benefits.

5.2   FIRM Risk Scorecard

The FIRM Risk Scorecard is a means of recording risk information in a structured manner. The FIRM Risk Scorecard records risks according to the main impact of the risk. It has four headings and the nature of the risks placed under each of the four headings is described in Table 3. An illustration of the risk capacity under each heading is shown in Figure 6.

The four headings of the FIRM Risk Scorecard offer a classification system for risks to the key dependencies in the organisation. These headings are as follows:

F   Financial
I   Infrastructure
R   Reputational
M   Marketplace

The FIRM approach allows risks to be classified as internal (financial and infrastructure) or external (reputational and marketplace). Also, the risks may be considered as mainly quantitative and so easy to quantify (financial and marketplace) or mainly qualitative and more difficult to quantify (infrastructure and reputational).

Although infrastructure and reputational risks may sometimes be difficult to quantify, all risks need to be evaluated in terms of the impact that could result if the risk materialises. Methods for the quantification of risks are discussed later. Figure 6 illustrates the control acceptance, hazard tolerance and opportunity appetite components of risk capacity under each heading of the FIRM Risk Scorecard. The way in which these component parts of the risk capacity can be calculated is discussed in later chapters. Note that the FIRM

Risk Scorecard is initially a means of illustrating risk capacity, as agreed by the board. It can also be used to record individual values at risk, as a means of comparing the actual risk exposure with the agreed risk capacity.

Appendix B uses the example of Whitechapel Football Club. This football club is presumed to make profits of £40 million per annum and have a market capitalisation of £100 million. The benchmark values for significant risks are 5% of profit (or an immediate impact of £2 million) and/or 10% of future earnings potential. This latter figure represents a reduction of 10% in the share price or an anticipated future earnings impact of £10 million. It is likely that the benchmark of a £2 million immediate impact can be readily applied to financial and marketplace headings. The benchmark of a £10 million loss of future earnings can be applied to the infrastructure and reputational headings.

The FIRM Risk Scorecard acts as a template for undertaking the risk assessment activity. It can be used as a structure to facilitate the identification of risks to the mission, corporate objectives, stakeholder expectations and key dependencies. Indeed, the FIRM Risk Scorecard structure may also assist with the setting and recording of corporate objectives and stakeholder expectations which are identifiable under the headings of the FIRM Risk Scorecard.

The risks that will be illustrated using the FIRM Risk Scorecard must ultimately be linked, via key dependencies, to core processes. The FIRM Risk Scorecard is a means of illustrating the priority significant risks that are described in the risk register. It is an important benefit of the FIRM Risk Scorecard that the headings also provide a means of structuring and recording the key dependencies in the organisation. The fact that the structure of the FIRM Risk Scorecard can be used to record key dependencies has the important benefit that a matrix of risks can be produced in a format that is entirely compatible with the FIRM Risk Scorecard. The production and application of a risk matrix is discussed in chapter 9.

The FIRM Risk Scorecard approach has similarities with the audit universe approach adopted by internal auditors. One of the most important issues of concern for organisations is that they may fail to recognise all of the risks that they face. The FIRM Risk Scorecard is a means of reducing this danger, because of the structured analysis that the FIRM Risk Scorecard requires.

Remember that the FIRM Risk Scorecard is a risk recording tool that assists with the measurement of risk exposure, by illustrating the risk capacity of the organisation. This facilitates the completion of an overall risk assessment of the organisation. Almost certainly, there will be the potential to place a specific risk under more than one heading of the FIRM Risk Scorecard.

	Financial	Infrastructure	Reputational	Marketplace
Description	Risks that will impact the way in which money is managed and profitability is achieved	Risks that will impact the level of efficiency and dysfunction within the core processes	Risks that will impact desire of stakeholders to deal or trade and level of customer retention	Risks that will impact the level of stakeholder trade or expenditure and customer retention
Desired State	An effective and adequate system of internal financial management and control	An infrastructure that has NUDE and efficiently satisfies customer requirements	A reputation that ensures a positive image for the organisation with stakeholders	Adequate funding of activities and adequate ongoing income from the marketplace
Internal or External Risk	Internal	Internal	External	External
Quantifiable	Usually	Sometimes	Not always	Yes
Measurement or RPI	Gains and losses from internal financial control	Level of efficiency in processes and operations	Nature of publicity and effectiveness of marketing profile	Income from commercial and market activities
Performance Gap	PROCEDURES Failure of procedures to control internal financial risks	PROCESS Failure of processes to operate without dysfunction	PERCEPTION Failure to achieve the desired perception of the organisation	PRESENCE Failure to achieve required presence in the marketplace
Control Mechanisms	• CapEx standards • Internal Control • Delegation of Authority	• Process Control • Loss Control • Insurance and risk financing	• Marketing • Advertising • Reputation and brand protection	• Strategic plans • Business plans • Opportunity Assessment

Summary of attributes under each heading of the FIRM Risk Scorecard

Table 3: Attributes of the FIRM Risk Scorecard

Such risks should be placed under the heading of the FIRM Risk Scorecard where the impact would be greatest.

5.2.1 Financial Risks

The main features associated with the risks to be placed under the financial heading of the FIRM Risk Scorecard are:

- risks that can impact the way in which cash resources available to and/or received by the organisation are allocated and controlled

- financial risks that are associated with failure of procedures to mitigate losses and ensure correct allocation of cash resources

- risks where the aim is to achieve an adequate system of internal financial management and control

Table 3 describes the attributes of risks to be placed under the financial risks heading of the FIRM Risk Scorecard. These risks are related to internal aspects of the organisation and in particular, internal financial control. Usually, financial risks are readily quantifiable and can be measured in terms of the value of any losses and/or the value of lost opportunities resulting from inadequate internal control of finances.

The benchmark for a financial risk to be significant could be linked to the capital expenditure limit above which CEO authorisation is required. This is likely to be between £1 million and £5 million, or more, for large organisations. It is reasonable to use this approach, because the CEO should only get involved in the authorisation of significant sums of money. Details of CEO and other authorisation levels will be set out in the Delegation of Authority for the organisation.

Accountants and internal auditors have much experience relevant to the control of internal financial risks. One would expect the finance director to understand internal financial control issues and to feel comfortable in this area. It may be appropriate for the finance director to co-ordinate activity under this heading of the FIRM Risk Scorecard and provide support to the owners of the risk, key dependency and/or core process that may be impacted. Generally speaking, financial risks are managed using a set of internal financial control procedures. These are often produced as part of a document entitled "Managers' Control Responsibilities".

Failure to adequately control financial risks results from weaknesses in the procedures within the organisation. Poor management of these risks may result in a procedures gap for the organisation. Typical control mechanisms for financial risks are capital expenditure (CapEx) approval systems and internal financial control procedures and protocols, including the Delegation of Authority document already mentioned.

There will be a range of benefits associated with using the FIRM Risk Scorecard, as part of implementing the risk productivity approach. These benefits can be presented using the structure of the FIRM Risk Scorecard. Under the financial heading, the benefits will include:

- reduced cost of funding and capital
- better control of capex approvals
- increased profitability for organisation
- accurate financial risk reporting
- enhanced Corporate Governance

5.2.2 Infrastructure Risks

The main features associated with the risks to be placed under the infrastructure heading of the FIRM Risk Scorecard are:

- risks that can impact the level of efficiency within the normal or routine operations of the organisation
- infrastructure risks, associated with the failure of routine processes to operate without disruption or dysfunction
- risks where the aim is to achieve and maintain an infrastructure that will continue to efficiently satisfy customer requirements

The risks to be placed under the infrastructure heading of the FIRM Risk Scorecard are described in Table 3. These risks are internal to the organisation and they can be quantified, although this may not always be straight forward. Despite the fact that infrastructure risks are internal, they may also arise from failure of suppliers to support the infrastructure of the organisation and/or be associated with the failure of outsourced services provided by external suppliers.

Infrastructure risks correspond to the traditional area of operation of the insurance market. Infrastructure risks can be evaluated according to the level of disruption to normal operation that occurs when the risk materialises. The disruption and/or dysfunction results from risks impacting the key dependencies that support the infrastructure of the organisation. Key dependencies associated with the infrastructure include buildings, machinery, people and IT architecture.

In general, organisations will have a reasonable understanding of the level at which the impact to the infrastructure dependencies becomes significant. The benchmark applied will relate to the extent and duration of any inability to operate normally and/or efficiently. A more quantified basis for evaluation of infrastructure risks would be a consideration of the impact on future profitability or earnings potential. For a listed company, this decrease or increase in earnings potential would be reflected in the share price. A typical benchmark test of significance for infrastructure risks in the case of a listed company would be a 10% movement in the share price.

Insurance practitioners have the greatest experience of infrastructure dependencies, because these are normally hazard risks. The management of infrastructure risks is the responsibility of operational staff and the board director responsible for co-ordinating these risks will normally be the operations director or the production director. That director should provide support to the owners of the risk, the key dependency and/or the core process that may be impacted.

Failure to control infrastructure risks will result in poor performance and/or efficiency of processes within the organisation. Poor management of these risks may result in a process gap for the organisation. Typical control mechanisms for hazard type infrastructure risks include ensuring that there is appropriate resilience and duplication of resources in the infrastructure, loss control techniques and insurance.

There will be a range of benefits associated with using the FIRM Risk Scorecard, as part of implementing the risk productivity approach. These benefits can be presented using the structure of the FIRM Risk Scorecard. Under the infrastructure heading, the benefits will include:

- efficiency and competitive advantage
- achievement of the state of NUDE
- improved supplier and staff morale
- targeted risk and cost reduction
- reduced operating costs

5.2.3   Reputational Risks

The main features associated with the risks to be placed under the reputational heading of the FIRM Risk Scorecard are:

- risks that can impact the continuing desire of customers and partners to deal or trade with the organisation

- reputational risks associated with failure of the organisation to achieve the desired perception with staff, customers, business partners and other stakeholders

- risks where the aim is to achieve a reputation and profile that will ensure a positive image for the organisation and its trade brands

The risks to be placed under the reputational heading of the FIRM Risk Scorecard are external to the organisation and they cannot always be readily quantified, either in terms of the magnitude or likelihood of impact. The measurement of reputational risks can be difficult, although the indicator used could be related to the level and nature of any publicity. A more quantified basis for evaluation of reputational risks would be a consideration of the impact on future profitability or earnings potential. For a listed company this increase or decrease in earnings potential would be reflected in the share price.

Reputational risks are much wider than simply those that could impact the brand. Reputational risks include ethical behaviour, continuity of supply and legal compliance. In fact, this heading of the FIRM Risk Scorecard covers key dependencies and risks that have a very wide range. As stated, this heading is concerned with anything that would result in customers, suppliers and other stakeholders feeling less, or more, inclined to do business with or support the organisation.

The above definition and description relates mainly to the hazard risk aspects of reputational risks; there are also substantial opportunities associated with reputational risks. There is potential for the overall reputation of the organisation to be enhanced by publicity and this will assist with the achievement of corporate objectives and the fulfilment of stakeholder expectations. In the context of opportunity risks, the organisation should ensure that adequate and appropriate brand development and extension takes place. Any organisation with a strong brand will wish to diversify the products and services that are marketed using that brand.

For Government and other public service departments, the reputational risk component is fundamentally important. Schools, hospitals, local authorities, universities and government departments encounter difficulties when their reputation is damaged. If the reputation of a school becomes damaged, then parents will want their children to go to another school and/or residents may decide to move to another location. The public perception of the efficiency and efficacy of a government agency or authority are all seriously effected by adverse publicity.

The board level responsibility for reputation is not specifically allocated in most organisations. However, there are some organisations where the post of Brand Manager has been created. As brand and reputation become more important, the responsibility of the board needs to be made clear and a board member needs to be identified as responsible for brand and reputation. The identified board director should act as a support to the owners of the risk, key dependency and/or core process that may be impacted by the reputational risk under consideration.

Failure to control the hazard aspects of reputational risks will result in an unsatisfactory image for the organisation. Reputational risks are a developing area for the provision of insurance solutions. Poor management of these risks may result in a perception gap for the organisation. Typical control mechanisms for reputational risks include marketing, advertising and brand protection. The brand protection aspects will often rely heavily on the event management plans. This planning will ensure that the organisation can respond rapidly and appropriately to any high profile publicity (good or bad) that the organisation attracts.

There will be a range of benefits associated with using the FIRM Risk Scorecard, as part of implementing the risk productivity approach. These benefits can be presented using the structure of the FIRM Risk Scorecard. Under the reputation heading, the benefits will include:

- regulators satisfied
- improved utilisation of company brand
- enhanced shareholder value
- good reputation and publicity
- improved perception of organisation

5.2.4 Marketplace Risks

The main features associated with the risks to be placed under the marketplace (including commercial risks) heading of the FIRM Risk Scorecard are:

- risks that can impact the level of customer expenditure and the level of customer retention

- marketplace risks that are associated with failure of the organisation to achieve the required presence or level of revenue in the marketplace

- risks where the aim is to achieve an adequate level of ongoing income in line with, or exceeding, the budget projections

Table 3 provides further information on the types of risks to be placed under the marketplace heading of the FIRM Risk Scorecard. Marketplace risks include the commercial risks faced by trading organisations. These risks are external to the organisation and can be quantified. The measurement of marketplace risks may be related to revenue levels and the cost of commercial activities. For non-commercial organisations, failure to achieve the desired marketplace impact would be a very important issue, even though there is no intention to undertake commercial or trading activities. Charities, for example, need to maintain a high marketplace presence in order to continue to stage successful fund raising activities.

Organisations will have a good level of understanding of their tolerance to marketplace hazard risks. The organisation should also be able to determine the level of appetite for marketplace opportunity risks. The appetite for opportunity risks will be related to the value that the organisation is willing to put at risk in order to undertake, for example, a new product launch or to introduce a new means of raising revenue in the marketplace.

The commercial director is likely to be the main board director with responsibility for core processes related to sales and marketing operations. Accordingly, the commercial director is the most able person to co-ordinate the management of these risks, and identify the risk owners. That director should then act as a support to the owners of the risk, key dependency and/or core process that may be impacted.

Marketplace risks will be mainly commercial for those organisations that sell services or products. For other organisations, such as charities, these will be the risks related to the ability to raise funds in the marketplace. Failure to control these risks will result in inadequate sales or funds for the organisation. Poor management of these risks may result in a presence gap for the organisation. Typical control mechanisms for marketplace risks include the structured and monitored development of business strategy and the introduction of procedures to undertake opportunity assessment of new business activities and proposals.

There will be a range of benefits associated with using the FIRM Risk Scorecard, as part of implementing the risk productivity approach. These benefits can be presented using the structure of the FIRM Risk Scorecard. Under the marketplace heading, the benefits will include:

- commercial opportunities maximised
- better marketplace presence
- increased customer spend, and satisfaction
- higher level of business successes
- lower level of business disasters

5.3   Risk Capacity

Most organisations make adequate profits, but take too much risk and/or make inappropriate use of the risk capacity of the organisation. Figure 6 is an illustration of the consolidated risk capacity of an organisation. It shows the level of risk that the board is willing to take under each of the headings of the FIRM Risk Scorecard. Risk capacity is not the same as the cumulative total of all of the individual values at risk associated with the risks facing the organisation. This cumulative total is the risk exposure of the organisation.

Risk capacity is the total value of the corporate resources that the board of the organisation is willing to put at risk. The risk capacity is the sum of hazard tolerance plus control acceptance plus opportunity appetite. Risk capacity represents a component of the overall resources of the organisation, as mentioned in chapter 1. Most organisations have not determined the value that it should have at risk (risk capacity) nor calculated how much value is actually at risk (risk exposure).

Underpinning the current level of interest in risk management is the idea that risk is a single transferable commodity within the organisation. If this is true, then an organisation should be able to decide how much it wishes to put at risk. The purpose of agreeing risk capacity is to ensure that the organisation does not put too much, or too little, value at risk. It may be acceptable for the organisation to have a total risk exposure that is greater than the risk capacity, provided that there are uncorrelated risks in the portfolio of significant risks. This analysis requires a level of sophistication that is not explored in detail in this book.

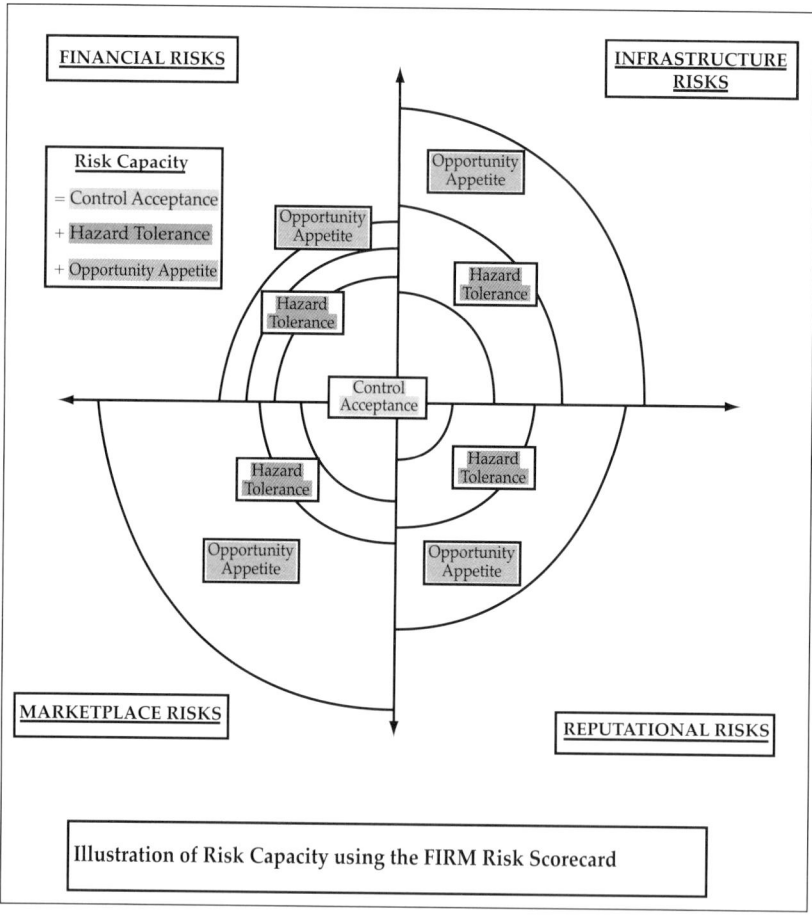

Illustration of Risk Capacity using the FIRM Risk Scorecard

Figure 6: FIRM Risk Scorecard

The organisation is unlikely to have equal risk capacity under each of the four headings of the FIRM Risk Scorecard. The risk capacity of the organisation needs to be fully utilised to ensure that it is used to maximum benefit. Similarly, the organisation should not put more value at risk than is appropriate, given the sector in which it operates and the prevailing market conditions. Fully utilising and correctly allocating risk capacity will help achieve risk productivity. Note that the risk capacity relates to the agreed allocation of values at risk and not the anticipated values of the range of possible outcomes. The value of the outcomes is influenced by the application of risk management tools and techniques to the CASE that materialise after the agreed value has been put at risk.

Summary and Review of Chapter 5

Section 1 sets out some of the basic issues for consideration in relation to the timescale for the impact of risks. Short term, medium term and long term risks are identified. Different organisations will allocate different timescales to long term, medium term and short term impact, depending on the size and nature of the organisation. Typically, the long term horizon is 1 to 5 years, the medium term horizon is within 12 months and the short term horizon is immediate.

It is important to recognise the full extent of the definition of risk, so that a fully integrative approach can be developed for the organisation. Identifying risk capacity as a single commodity that can be deliberately allocated is vital, if full benefit is to be obtained from the risks that the organisation decides to take.

Section 2 introduces the FIRM Risk Scorecard as a valuable tool for demonstrating the inter-dependent nature of risk and the integrative nature of risk management. Table 3 sets out the main attributes of risks that would be placed under each of the headings of the FIRM Risk Scorecard. The headings of the FIRM Risk Scorecard are:

- **Financial**
- **Infrastructure**
- **Reputational**
- **Marketplace**

Recognising the nature of the risks to be included within the FIRM Risk Scorecard enables easier understanding of many of the ideas and concepts supporting the risk productivity approach. At any one time the FIRM Risk Scorecard can facilitate illustration of the risk capacity of the organisation and allow the risk capacity to be compared with the actual risk exposure. Decisions can then be made on how the risk capacity will be allocated, in a way that provides maximum benefit to the organisation.

The main message from this chapter is that the FIRM Risk Scorecard ensures robust risk assessment. The FIRM Risk Scorecard can be used to illustrate risk capacity as in Figure 6. Case Study 5 consolidates the key messages outlined in this chapter.

Case Study 5: Personal Risk Profile – (Part 1)

This case study considers the application of the FIRM Risk Scorecard approach to the risks that could impact personal core processes. The question of how personal risk capacity is allocated is explored in this case study. Consider the personal circumstances of Russell Square.

Russell has undertaken an analysis of his personal mission, the stakeholders in his life and their expectations of him. He has also set himself personal objectives. One of the core processes that he has identified is the "earning a living" process. A key dependency is transport and one of the risks that could impact his transport arrangements is an unreliable car. Accordingly, Russell has decided to use some of the risk capacity in his FIRM Risk Scorecard to buy a replacement car.

The budget for purchasing a car can be constructed by considering his hazard tolerance, control acceptance and opportunity appetite in respect of this key dependency that supports the "earning a living" core process. Together, these define his annual risk capacity for buying and running a car.

Hazard Tolerance:	£500 breakdown/repairs
	£500 insurance excess/deductible
Control Acceptance:	£500 servicing cost
	£1,000 insurance premium
Opportunity Appetite:	£3,000 purchase payments p/a
	£1,000 annual depreciation
Risk Capacity:	**£6,500 per annum**

In summary, Russell has decided that he is able to afford a car that will cost him £1,500 per annum in respect of insurance + servicing (control acceptance) and purchase payments + an anticipated £1,000 in depreciation (opportunity appetite) and a willingness to spend up to a further £1,000 on breakdown/repair and insurance excess (hazard tolerance).

When selecting the car that he will buy, Russell must be sure that it does not represent an actual risk exposure that is in excess of his risk capacity, because for example the car that he selects is too big or too old. Also, he will realise that, by using risk capacity to purchase a car, he will have less resources, and less risk capacity, available to be utilised elsewhere.

6 Identification of Significant Risks

A risk is significant if it could impact above the benchmark level for significance and thereby threaten the existence of the organisation

This chapter suggests methods for the identification of significant risks that could impact the mission of an organisation. When an organisation wishes to identify the significant risks that it faces, a methodology is required. Available methodologies include the collection of information on the top ten risks facing each department or division. Risk mapping and risk dependency techniques can also be used. Alternatively, an analysis of stakeholder expectations and/or key dependencies can be undertaken.

Apart from recognising when a risk is significant, there is also a need to identify which of the significant risks should be treated as the priority significant risks. Techniques for ranking risks are well established, but there is also a need to decide what scope exists for further improving control. Consideration of the scope for further improvement allows clear identification of the priority significant risks.

A risk is significant if it could have a magnitude in excess of the benchmark test for significance for that type of risk. The identification of potentially significant risks will be undertaken during a risk ranking exercise. It is necessary to decide:

- the magnitude of the impact of the risk
- the likelihood of it materialising at or above that magnitude
- the scope for further improvement in control

This will lead to the identification of the priority significant risks. Most organisations will find that the number of priority significant risks faced by the organisation is between ten and twenty.

6.1. Risk Recognition

In order to ensure a robust risk management approach, accurate risk recognition and risk ranking is required. The four headings of the FIRM Risk Scorecard can be used as the framework for identifying the risks faced by an organisation. The production of a risk matrix to aid risk recognition is discussed later in this chapter. The fundamental requirement of any system of risk recognition is that all potentially significant risks are identified.

A number of approaches are available when undertaking a risk recognition or risk identification exercise. Methodologies for the identification of significant risks include approaches based on:

- analysis of corporate objectives
- analysis of stakeholder expectations
- risk mapping techniques
- analysis of key dependencies
- top ten risks from each department
- CEO opinion

The outcome of a risk assessment exercise for the organisation is the risk profile of the organisation. The risk profile can be recorded and presented as a risk register. It will set out details of the priority significant risks faced by the organisation. The risk register will also contain details of the measurements that will be used to monitor the performance of each priority significant risk. These risk based measurements are labelled as risk productivity indicators or RPIs.

Options for the risk recognition stage include workshops, a series of one on one interviews and the use of audience voting software. Increasingly, the use of "chat-room" type technology is becoming common. This allows delegates at a virtual conference to anonymously put forward ideas and comments onto a computer information base. Ideas appear on all delegates' screens and comments are exchanged. This leads to a common view of the risk priorities.

It is vitally important that everybody involved in the production of the risk profile recognises that there is a difference between risks and management issues. There is a temptation for a workshop or a series of interviews to produce a list of the top management issues facing the organisation, rather than a list of the priority significant risks. Remember that a risk must be stated as a circumstance, action, situation or event (CASE).

For example, the decision to expand into (e.g.) Russia may be one of the strategies to be followed by the organisation. This expansion plan is likely to be a top management issue and one of the most important corporate objectives. Describing the failure to successfully expand into Russia as a key risk is too vague and unhelpful. The CASE that could impact the expansion plan are the risks to the strategy but the strategy itself should not be described as a risk. Describing failure to expand into Russia as a risk would provide a high level statement that is impossible to analyse in a structured manner.

Expansion into Russia will only be successful if certain key dependencies are present. These key dependencies can be identified and listed. Risks will impact these key dependencies and the risks can be collected by the use of a risk matrix, as described later. The hazard risks that could impact the key dependencies are likely to include the following:

> Failure to find a suitable location

> Refusal of planning consent

> Inability to recruit trained staff

> Joint Venture partners not available

6.1.1 Corporate Objectives

Corporate objectives are often used as the starting point for a risk recognition exercise. However, the attempt to move directly from a consideration of corporate objectives to a clear identification of priority significant risks is filled with dangers. The first problem is that corporate objectives are often not fully stated. If they are fully stated, they will often be quoted as high level strategic objectives that do not address all aspects of the corporate core processes.

If the corporate objectives are not fully stated then an alternative starting point for risk identification could be the mission statement, although this may also be too high level to successfully attach risks. The mission statement will be a high level statement of why the organisation exists. The mission statement is helpful, because it implies the measurements that the organisation will use to determine whether it is being successful.

Despite the dangers, corporate objectives are often used as the basis for risk recognition. The question to be asked in respect of each corporate objective, and the mission statement, is "what could impact the achievement of this objective". The question can be asked within a number of structures or approaches. Remember that a full statement of objectives would set out the operational, change and strategic objectives of the organisation. The corporate objectives could be identified and set out within the framework of the FIRM Risk Scorecard.

Each objective could be analysed to identify hazard risks, control risks and opportunity risks as separate questions. Alternatively and additionally, each objective could be analysed to identify the financial, infrastructure, reputational and marketplace risks, again as separate questions. This multiple questions approach provides the best means of ensuring that the organisation does not fail to recognise all of the risks that it faces.

6.1.2   Stakeholder Expectations

Business process redesign specialists recommend an approach based on the analysis of stakeholder expectations, because it represents a very robust methodology. The risk productivity approach described in this book is based on the analysis of stakeholder expectations as the best way of identifying the key dependencies for the organisation and then the priority significant risks that could impact those key dependencies.

Analysis of stakeholder expectations leads to the identification of the core processes within the organisation. Analysis of the stakeholder expectations and/or core processes can then be used as the basis for a detailed risk assessment. The danger exists that seeking to attach risks directly to stakeholder expectations and/or core processes may be too high level for the successful recognition of risks.

Having identified the stakeholders and their expectations, the core processes that deliver those expectations can then be analysed. Again the question "what could impact the operation of these core processes" or "what could impact the delivery of these stakeholder expectations" needs to be asked. Each process could be analysed to identify hazard risks, control risks and opportunity risks as separate questions.

Alternatively and additionally, each process could be analysed to identify the financial, infrastructure, reputational and marketplace risks, again as separate questions.

6.1.3 Risk Mapping

A number of risk mapping software tools are now available. These are based on an analysis of the risks or an analysis of the decision making procedures within the organisation. The use of software will require a structured approach that will, in itself, prove useful, because of the logical and structured discussions that are necessary in undertaking the analysis.

Software tools have been developed that can assist with the identification of the dependencies within the organisation. Generally speaking, the mission statement and/or the corporate objectives are established. Then, the key dependencies that must be present in order to achieve the mission and/or each objective are identified. The analysis of each dependency identifies further dependencies that must be present in order to support that key dependency. This analysis continues until the sub-dependency is outside the control of the organisation, the sub-dependency is measurable, or further analysis is not helpful.

Quantitative values can be inserted into the computer model regarding the frequency and duration with which each risk is expected to materialise, and in turn impact each of the key dependencies. The cost, or benefit, of the CASE materialising together with the ongoing cost, or benefit, per hour that the CASE continues to be present and/or have its impact can be included in the model. By undertaking this analysis, a clear understanding of the impact of the identified circumstances, actions, situations or events (CASE) can be quantified within the risk map.

One of the main advantages of this approach is that it produces a computer model for further evaluation and amendment. Also, a better understanding of the organisation is invariably achieved. The task can, however, be time consuming and it is sometimes hampered by the shortage of reliable statistical information.

6.1.4   Key Dependencies

Risk mapping is, in effect, a computerised version of key dependency analysis. However, the technique is worthy of further consideration. This section comments on the identification of key dependencies as a separate issue, so that the idea of a risk matrix can be introduced and discussed. A key dependency is something that must be present to support a core process. The key dependencies may be internal or external to the organisation and may be financial or non-financial.

The stakeholder expectations should be fully identified and the core processes that deliver these expectations should be fully established by the organisation. The key dependencies that support the core processes can be recognised, using the structure of the FIRM Risk Scorecard. A risk matrix can then be produced and Table 7 in chapter 9 provides an example of a partially populated risk matrix.

The benefit of using the key dependencies approach is that it builds on the related ideas of stakeholder expectations and core processes. This approach will provide the most holistic means of identifying the priority significant risks facing the organisation. The approach is robust and well structured, although it is likely to be time consuming.

Note that each dependency is likely to have three components. There will be a portion of the dependency that is held in reserve, a further portion that represents revenue or routine expenditure and the final portion that is at risk. This final portion relates to the concepts of value at risk and risk capacity. It is the at risk portion that will benefit most from the application of risk management tools and techniques. However, attempting to manage the "at risk" portion of the key dependency separated from the remainder of the key dependency will result in confusion and failure.

This approach will also tend to separate risks from the context that gave rise to the risks. For example, a transport company will need to keep its vehicles in service. One of the reasons that vehicles will be out of service is road traffic accidents. Managing the road traffic accident aspect of the fleet separate from other fleet management issues will cause confusion and it will be unsuccessful.

More change means a greater need for business development. In times of change, an organisation will have to put more of the reserve and revenue portions of a key dependency at risk, in order to keep up with the competition. In other words, change and uncertainty creates greater risk. Take the example of a car manufacturer with a wide range of models for sale. Some models may be classic models that will continue to sell for years ahead and these are the reserve part of the range of models. Other models will provide routine, predictable levels of revenue into the medium term. The final models may be suffering from declining sales and need to be replaced. The replacement of these declining models requires allocation of risk capacity, in the form of opportunity appetite.

Greater change in customer expectations means more product development and more corporate resources or value put at risk. If too much of a key dependency is at risk, or has to be put at risk, then an organisation should take steps to reduce that risk. Those steps may include joint ventures to launch new products, or the testing of new products in selected geographical markets only.

The aim of the key dependency analysis is to collect as much relevant information as possible. As with collection of information for risk mapping, this can often take place during a workshop. With improvements in software and communications, workshops can be undertaken as virtual workshops with participants taking part in a "chat-room" environment. This will also enable contributions to be made anonymously from remote locations. Such anonymous contributions ensure that all comments are given the same weight and importance.

6.1.5   Top Ten Risks from each Department

An apparently simple way of collecting risk information is to ask each department in the organisation to submit details of the top ten risks facing the department. The main difficulty with this approach is that the different departments may use different methods and/or different criteria for deciding risk priorities. There are several advantages to this approach. The main advantage is that responsibility for assessing the risks remains with the department. Therefore, there is a greater chance that the department will retain ownership of the risks and retain responsibility for any risk improvement recommendations that they decide are necessary.

The risks reported by the different departments will need to be consolidated at head office. In order to overcome the difficulty of consolidating the results from several departments into a risk register for the whole organisation, the departments could be given a populated risk matrix. This will facilitate more consistent descriptions of the risks reported by departments, the risks can then be allocated to the appropriate place in the risk matrix, for easier consolidation. There is a danger, however, that the department will ignore any risk not included in the sample risk matrix.

Care should be taken throughout the exercise to ensure that each department understands that it retains ownership of the risks. In outline, the procedure for collecting details of the top risks facing each department and ensuring the subsequent improved management of those risks will be as follows:

- request that each division identifies its top ten risks
- consolidate the answers using the structure of a risk matrix
- identify the significant risks to organisation
- allocate RPIs to the priority significant risks
- notify the departments of the RPIs
- obtain action plans from the departments
- monitor the risk productivity indicators (RPIs)
- review the risk management protocols

One of the major disadvantages of collecting information on this "bottom up" basis is that the individual departments will tend to understate the importance of risks external to the organisation. This disadvantage is inherent to this approach and can only be overcome by head office, where the departmental responses are consolidated. It will be for the person or group consolidating the departmental results at head office to ensure that all head office specialist colleagues are consulted. These specialist colleagues will include tax, insurance, corporate treasury specialists etc. In this way, the evaluation of the internal CASE, as reported, will take place at the same time as appropriate emphasis is placed on external CASE.

6.1.6   CEO Opinion

The chief executive officer (CEO) has ultimate responsibility for risk management. Also, the CEO should have the best informed opinion of the external risks facing the organisation. The direct involvement of the CEO in the risk identification phase is vital but the bias of the CEO towards external risks needs to be overcome. It is, after all, the function of the CEO to look outwards from the organisation, so an external bias is understandable. The external risks that will receive high rating by the CEO will relate mainly to the reputational and marketplace headings of the FIRM Risk Scorecard.

Although the CEO must be involved in the exercise of compiling the risk register, there is a substantial danger that the CEO will put forward a view that is expected to prevail. If a risk matrix has been produced then this should be shared with the CEO to demonstrate that the organisation also faces significant internal issues. The CEO may need educating in the full range of risks that can be present, so that a better informed and balanced opinion is offered.

The main advantage of significant input from the CEO is that it shows buy-in at the most senior level. In some organisations the CEO may be the ultimate barrier to enhanced risk management because of the cavalier approach of many CEOs towards risk, especially the taking of opportunity risks.

6.2. Significant Risks

The identification of the priority significant risks facing an organisation can be undertaken using the following steps:

1. If the risk has high or very high magnitude in relation to the benchmark test for significance, then it is potentially significant

2. If the risk has a high or very high likelihood of materialising at or above the benchmark level, then it is confirmed as significant

3. If there is high or very high scope for cost effective improvement in control, then the risk is a priority significant risk

Generally speaking, it is only the priority significant risks that require attention at the most senior level in the organisation. Except that, it is appropriate that regulatory risks also receive boardroom attention, especially in relation to health and safety issues. However, in practice, the board will expect these regulatory risks to be properly managed and the board will only receive routine reports describing risk performance or, a special report if a specific issue has arisen.

A risk is a potentially significant risk if it could impact above the benchmark level for significance and thereby threaten the future existence of the organisation in its present size and form. A significant risk would have the ability or potential to impact, inhibit, enhance or cause doubt over, the key dependencies that support the core processes of the organisation.

It is likely that each core process will be the responsibility of a board director. It is also likely that each of the key dependencies supporting the core process will be the responsibility of a manager. The manager of the key dependency is almost certain to be the owner of the risk or risks that could impact that key dependency. Where risks within outsourced or supplier organisations are concerned, it is likely that a manager will be responsible for the management of the external contract that relates to that key dependency. That manager will have responsibility for managing the consequences of any risk materialising within the supplier organisation that could impact the (outsourced) key dependency.

Significant risks will have the ability to impact above a benchmark level. This benchmark approach is better than using the top ten risks approach. A test for significance is vital, because it is not sensible for an organisation to work on the basis that only ten risks (or some other arbitrary number of risks) will be significant and that others can be ignored. By using the top ten risks approach, it is possible that some significant risks could be ignored. Conversely, management effort will be wasted if only five significant risks exist within the organisation and ten risks are being scrutinised at boardroom level.

The benchmark should be set at a level that represents a significant impact for the organisation. Typically, this benchmark level will be an impact of 5% profit and/or a 10% change in future earnings capability. The later benchmark test will materialise as a 10% movement in the share price for a listed company. Benchmarks will vary between organisations and the same risk will have different benchmarks attached in different organisations.

Consider the example of non-availability of suitably qualified staff being a priority significant risk. An organisation in the media sector may face an annual increase of 10% in staff costs and staff turnover of 20% per annum. In this case, the risks associated with staff turnover, staff costs and the availability of suitably qualified staff may be managed to a satisfactory level, even at those high cost and high turnover levels. This level of staff turnover and cost inflation may be acceptable, despite the fact that for an organisation in the engineering sector, this level of risk performance would undermine the continued existence of the organisation.

6.2.1   Risk Matrix

Production of a risk matrix requires the identification of the following information:

- the key dependencies under each of the four headings of the FIRM Risk Scorecard

- the timescale over which the risks may impact, as short term, medium term or long term risks

- the individual risks that may arise, leading to population of the risk matrix

Table 7 in Chapter 9 provides an example of a partially populated risk matrix, specifically in relation to a football club. Such a risk matrix can also act as an aide memoir to facilitate the undertaking of a risk assessment by individual departments. The matrix sets out the key dependencies using the structure of the FIRM Risk Scorecard. The matrix provides a checklist of risks as short term, medium term and long term. Hazard risks, control risks and opportunity risks are all included in the sample risk matrix. The approach that combines hazard risks, control risks and opportunity risks in the same matrix may be too holistic an approach for some organisations, but consolidating all risks into a single matrix should remain the ultimate goal. As a starting point, such organisations should begin the process by concentrating on hazard risks only.

Although the identification of significant risks may be time consuming, the staff within the organisation will know the answers. The role of the risk manager is to facilitate the task of compiling the list. A common understanding of circumstance, action, situation or event (CASE) will be necessary. The matrix must be populated with the risks, rather the management issues facing the organisation or department. A simple question to ask to confirm that the matrix is populated with risks and not management issues is "can each item that is listed be attached directly to an identifiable event". Remember that it is the events that are the risks.

6.2.2   Risk Significance

It is worth establishing a few rules for the identification of the priority significant risks facing the organisation. The first important point to note is that each risk should be considered at its current value or level. Estimation of the inherent risk value will assist with the calculation of the corporate resources being used to control the risk, but the current level is the more important issue to consider when compiling the risk register. The risk register is, after all, a snapshot in time.

The questions to be asked about a risk are:

1.   What is the current risk magnitude (M)

2.   Does that magnitude exceed the benchmark test for significance

3.   What is the likelihood (L) of the risk materialising at the benchmark

4.   What is the scope (S) for further improvement in control

If the magnitude (M) is high or very high in relation to the benchmark, then the risk is potentially significant. If the likelihood (L) is also high or very high, then the risk is confirmed as significant. If the scope (S) for further cost effective control is also high or very high, then the risk becomes a priority significant risk.

In relation to priority significant risks consider the example used in Appendix B. Whitechapel Football Club (Whitechapel FC) is presumed to make profits of £40 million per annum and have a market capitalisation of £100 million. The benchmark values for significant risks will be set by Whitechapel FC, but are likely to be 5% of profit, or an immediate impact of £2 million, and/or 10% of future earnings potential. The 10% impact on future earnings potential will be reflected in the share price and, therefore, the market capitalisation. The 10% impact on future earnings potential equates to an anticipated future impact of £10 million.

The £2 million immediate figure is likely to be used as the benchmark measurement for financial and marketplace risks and the 10% change in share price figure is likely to be the benchmark for infrastructure and reputational risks. As each individual CASE in the risk matrix is evaluated, the question can be asked "will this CASE impact at or above the benchmark of £2 million immediately and/or have an impact of 10% on the share price. If the answer to either question is yes, then the CASE is identified as potentially significant.

6.2.3 Risk Priorities

For a risk to become a priority significant risk, it will need to meet the criteria outlined above. The risk matrix will be populated with all of the risks that the brainstorming exercise has identified. Some of those risks will then be identified as potentially significant risks. At this point, each individual potentially significant risk will need to be assessed, in terms of magnitude (M), likelihood (L) and scope (S) for improved control. Note the following:

Magnitude (M) x Likelihood (L) = Risk Significance
Risk Significance x Scope (S)　= Risk Priority

Many organisations use a scoring system to assist with the prioritisation of risks. If a scoring system is to be used, then the same scoring system can be applied to magnitude, likelihood and scope, as follows:

Low = 1　　Medium = 2　　High = 3　　Very High = 4

Figure 7 (overleaf) shows the actual risk information for Whitechapel FC in a diagrammatical form. Figure 7 suggests that the priority significant risks can be represented in four boxes. These boxes identify the likely response to the risks placed in each of the boxes as follows:

Low significance　and　Low scope　= passive review
Low significance　and　High scope　= active interest
High significance　and　Low scope　= active review
High significance　and　High scope　= active improvement

As might be expected, Figure 7 shows no priority significant risks that are fully in the passive review or active interest areas for Whitechapel FC, since it is unlikely that the priority significant risks would score that low. The priority significant risks are divided between active review and active improvement. In this example, the four main priority significant risks are a combination of opportunity, control and hazard. They are also a mix of short term, medium term and long term. Figure 7 presents the risk information in a way that it is easy to understand and evaluate.

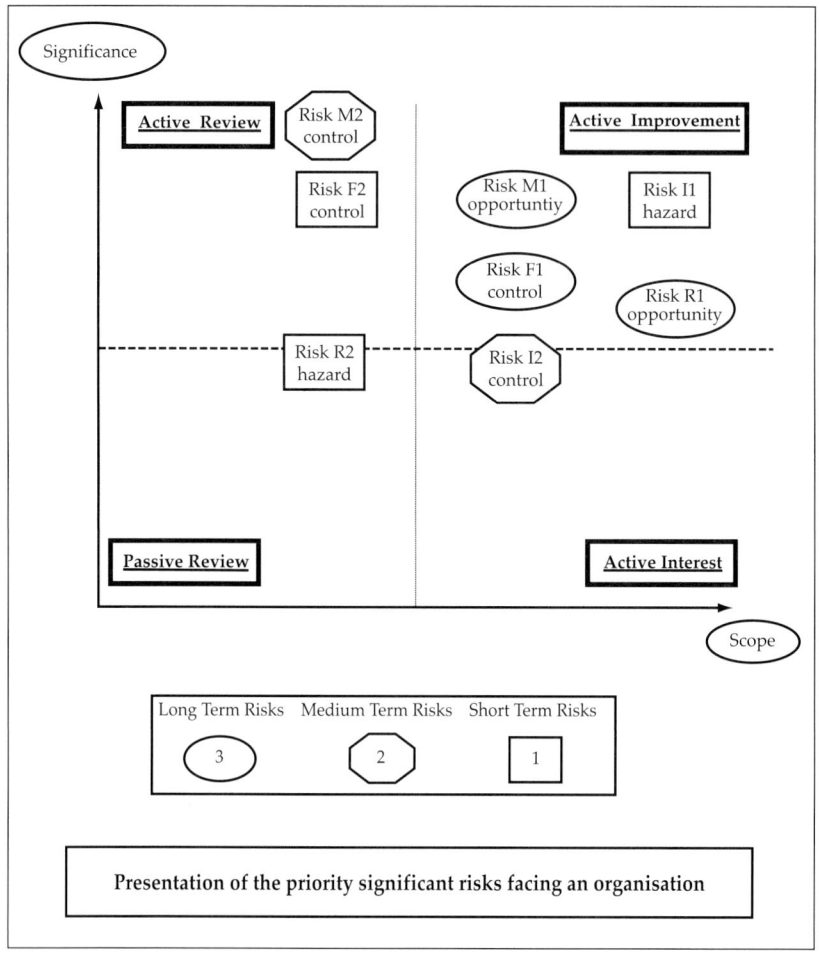

Figure 7: Presentation of Risk Priorities

Note that as a risk moves towards the top right corner of Figure 7, it represents an increasing amount of risk exposure for the organisation. By definition, each of the priority significant risks will put at least the benchmark value at risk. For Whitechapel FC, this is a £2 million immediate impact and/or a £10 million impact on future earnings potential. Using the £2 million immediate impact figure for each risk, the eight priority significant risks presented in Figure 7 may, therefore, represent a total value at risk of perhaps £20 million.

Additionally, there will be other risks that are not significant but cumulatively they will also add to the risk exposure. Assume that these non-significant risks represent a further £5 million of risk exposure, making a total current risk exposure of £25 million per annum. This calculation does not yet take account of whether the risks are correlated. If some of the risks have zero correlation with each other then the actual risk exposure per annum will be less than the £25 million unadjusted risk exposure figure.

Note that the analysis of risks set out above is focused on the current risk levels. These levels represent values at risk and the total of all of the values at risk is the current risk exposure of the organisation. It is unlikely that all of the risks will materialise in any one year, assuming that there is limited correlation between the risks. Therefore, the risk exposure, adjusted for correlation, will be less than the total of the values at risk. The risk capacity of the organisation is the value of corporate resources that the board has agreed should be put at risk. During the risk productivity exercise, the organisation will need to compare the current actual adjusted risk exposure with agreed risk capacity.

Using the unadjusted risk exposure information, Whitechapel FC needs to satisfy itself regarding several related questions:

1. Does Whitechapel FC wish to put £25 million at risk;

2. Is the board willing to declare a risk capacity of £25 million;

3. Is more or less than £25 million currently at risk;

4. Are the identified significant risks highly correlated

If the organisation has not agreed a figure for its risk capacity and/or if the adjusted for correlation current risk exposure differs from the £25 million optimal figure, then Whitechapel FC does not have sufficiently robust risk management protocols in place. Remember that Whitechapel FC will have reserve funds, revenue (or routine expenditure) and risk capacity. Other questions about the allocation of risk capacity can also be asked and these questions are explored in the consolidated case study in Appendix B.

The value at risk for each individual opportunity risk will be seen as an investment, but it is still part of the risk capacity of the organisation. In other words, the fact that the above analysis discusses values as risk does not imply that the risks are all hazard risks. All types of risk require that values be put at risk, although opportunity risks are accepted in anticipation of a net positive return. The analysis is based on the 99% certainty lines presented in Figure 3. Whitechapel FC can now start to analyse the total value at risk, its relationship to the risk capacity and current risk exposure of the organisation and the extent to which the cumulative range of possible outcomes (99%) are acceptable. The cumulative outcome will be the sum of the anticipated (99%) individual risk outcomes for each risk, as calculated from the possible range of outcomes similar to those illustrated in Figure 3.

At 99% certainty and the full risk capacity of £25 million at risk, the range of anticipated outcomes may range from a loss of £5 million to a profit of £100 million. For the sake of this analysis, the organisation is assumed to be working on the basis that if a risk has a less than 1 in 100 chance of happening then it will not materialise that year. There is only a 1 in 100 chance of being outside those limits. Therefore, in relation to the full risk portfolio of Whitechapel FC, there is a 1 in 200 chance of a worse outcome than a loss of £5 million and a 1 in 200 chance of an outcome that is better than a profit of £100 million.

6.2.4   Risk Analysis

There are a number of reasons for wanting to undertake a detailed analysis of the priority significant risks. The organisation needs to agree a common understanding of each risk and its importance to the organisation. This will lead to agreement on the actions that should be taken to further improve the management of that risk.

Table 4 overleaf suggests the extent of the analysis that should be undertaken for each priority significant risk. This may be too detailed an analysis for some organisations. In that case, the organisation need only analyse each risk to the extent that is helpful. By undertaking a detailed analysis of each risk, the appropriate risk productivity indicators (RPIs) can be identified.

The main headings used in Table 4 identify the range of information that should be recorded about each of the priority significant risks. In simple terms, the information in Table 4 relates to:

1. Risk Title and   — Common understanding of the risk, its
   Description   possible impacts and consequences

2. Core Process and   — Context within which the risk exists in
   Dependency   the organisation

3. Current Risk Status — Level of risk magnitude, likelihood, scope for improvement and value at risk

4. Risk Control Measures — Resources allocated to controlling the risk and proposed further controls

5. Required level of Risk Performance — RPIs to be attached to the risk to ensure satisfactory future risk performance

---

1. Risk Title and Description:
- Risk Name and Risk Index:
- Risk Impact and Risk Type:
- Description of Risk:
- Consequences of the risk materialising:

2. Core Process and Dependency:
- Core Process that may be impacted:
- Description of Core Process:
- Specific Activity or Dependency that may be impacted:
- Dependency (and Risk) owned by:

3. Current Risk Status:
- Current Risk Magnitude:
- Current Risk Likelihood:
- Scope for further improvement:
- Current Risk Exposure (Value at Risk):

4. Risk Control Measures:
- Existing Controls and corporate resources allocated:
- Recommended further controls:
- Responsibility for implementing further controls:
- Arrangements (Audit Plans) to ensure implementation:

5. Required Level of Risk Performance:
- Value of Risk to be allocated in future:
- Key Performance Indicators (KPIs) for the core process:
- Risk Productivity Indicators (RPIs) for the risk:
- Comments on future Risk Performance:

Suggested content for the detailed analysis of priority significant risks

Table 4: Analysis of Significant Risks

6.2.5   Risk Register

The suggested format for the front index page of a risk register is shown in Table B2 in Appendix B. The full risk register will contain details of the analysis of each of the priority significant risks, including information on the risk productivity indicators (RPIs) allocated to each risk. The risk register should be considered as a snapshot in time, just like the balance sheet of the organisation. It is helpful for the organisation to view the risk register as a snapshot. This approach reinforces the view that risks are dynamic and changing.

The corporate risk register should only contain details of the priority significant risks facing the organisation. The departmental risk registers will contain detailed information on the full range of significant risks faced by each department. The production of a corporate risk register will enable an organisation to keep track of its priority significant risks and ensure that each risk is managed throughout the lifecycle of the risk.

Information on each priority significant risk will need to be kept until the risk is retired. The risk may retire or cease to be significant because processes have changed, the risk has been controlled to below significant level or the risk has been eliminated. There may, however, be dangers associated with producing a risk register. The risks may become separated from the situation that gave rise to the risk. The risk register should, therefore, be viewed as a corporate monitoring tool to be used by the board and the audit committee. It should not be shared with the departments or risk owners, unless it can be shared without reducing local ownership of the risks.

There is also a danger that the risk register will become a static record of actions pending. Risk management should be a dynamic input into the successful management of the organisation. Therefore, the risk register should be updated dynamically and frequently. More importantly, the actions required to improve the management of individual risks should be embedded into routine management actions.

6.3   Utilising Risk Capacity

An organisation needs to ensure that there is sufficient utilisation of the risk capacity of the organisation. It also needs to be satisfied that it is not putting too much of its resources at risk by having an unacceptably high cumulative risk exposure. There are dangers associated with taking too much risk and also dangers associated with not taking enough risk. It is probably the case that even the most profitable and successful organisations have too much of the corporate resources at risk, without recognising that fact and taking appropriate actions to adequately manage the risks.

Risk exposure is the sum of the values at risk in respect of each of the significant risks faced by the organisation. An organisation should be able to decide how much of its current profit and/or future earning potential it wishes to put at risk. An organisation needs to establish and agree the correct balance of reserves to revenue to risk. The significant risks need to be analysed to determine the actual values at risk. This analysis can be facilitated and recorded using the FIRM Risk Scorecard. Total risk exposure can exceed risk capacity provided that some of the risks are not correlated. This will be a substantial and sophisticated calculation.

The analysis, using the FIRM Risk Scorecard, will enable the organisation to decide if certain amounts of the risk capacity under one or more heading of the FIRM Risk Scorecard are under utilised, whilst too much risk capacity is allocated elsewhere. Some of the risks may then be identified as being over managed, either individually, or as a group of risks under one heading of the FIRM Risk Scorecard.

Take the example of Holborn Chemical Transport Limited (HCT). HCT is the chemical transport company used in the case studies in this chapter and in chapter 8. There will be a large amount of risk capacity that needs to be used on operational hazard risks. HCT has identified an opportunity based on offering customers the outsourced service of HCT managing the customers' own on-site bulk chemical storage facility. The board needs to ask whether Holborn Chemical Transport Limited has enough risk capacity available to allocate to the development and provision of these new activities. If this business development is not fully evaluated, HCT could find that it has exceeded its risk capacity and is suffering too much risk exposure. This evaluation ensures that HCT fully understands the implications of actions that alter its risk profile. Case study 8 explores this example in more detail.

Summary and Review of Chapter 6

Section 1 discussed mechanisms for the identification of priority significant risks. The approach is based on the use of the FIRM Risk Scorecard as a framework for the recognition of risks. A key area of concern for many organisations is that they may fail to recognise all of the risks that could impact the core processes in the organisation. The FIRM Risk Scorecard is a means of reducing the chances that potentially significant risks are not identified.

Similar exercises can be undertaken to identify the hazard risks, control risks and opportunity risks that could impact the core processes in the organisation. The FIRM Risk Scorecard approach can be used to facilitate the identification of all three types of risk.

Section 2 discussed the fact that the identification of significant risks cannot be undertaken in isolation from the processes that could be impacted by the risks. It is suggested that it is important to establish the benchmark for risk significance for the organisation. This analysis will deliver the additional benefit that the core processes that are most at risk will also be identified. This is discussed in more detail in Appendix B.

The production and population of a risk matrix is suggested as a means of structuring the risk recognition phase. The structure of the risk matrix will help to reduce the chances of the organisation applying the risk productivity approach to too many risks. This can be described as "risk overload".

The main message from this chapter is that there is a need for a benchmark to be established that will be the test of whether a risk is potentially significant. Also, the level of risk analysis required by the organisation needs to be decided, based on the approach suggested in Table 4. Case Study 6 consolidates the key messages outlined in this chapter.

Case Study 6: Chemical Road Tankers – (Part 1)

This case study concerns Holborn Chemical Transport Limited (HCT), a chemical tanker company in the business of transporting and delivering all types of bulk chemicals, including hazardous chemicals. The core process "timely and safe delivery of bulk chemicals" fulfils one of the main stakeholder expectations. Several stakeholders, including customers, regulatory bodies, the police, tanker drivers etc. share this expectation.

The key dependencies of this core process include adequate health and safety standards and procedures. There are several CASE that could impact this key dependency. These CASE are mainly hazard risks and they need to be managed as part of the management of this "continuity and monitoring of routine operations" type core process.

The risks that could impact the key dependency of adequate health and safety standards, include the following:

- uncontrolled chemical spillage
- serious motor accident
- failure to follow procedures
- defective safety equipment

The above list identifies the risks that could impact the key dependency that supports this core process. HCT now needs to decide which of these risks are potentially significant. This can be done by establishing the benchmark test for significance under the infrastructure heading of the FIRM Risk Scorecard. Holborn Chemicals Limited has decided that the benchmark test for significance is £250,000. This benchmark would be reached if a CASE could cause "uncontrolled and/or uncontained spillage or loss of more than 100Kg of hazardous chemical", because such an incident would be expected to lead to total costs in excess of £250,000.

The organisation will be able to set a maximum acceptable frequency for each CASE that could cause that type of incident. It is likely that the measurement will be related to incidents per million miles driven and/or incidents per thousand deliveries and/or incidents per thousand tanker hose pipe connections. The selected measurements will be some of the risk productivity indicators (RPIs) applied to the "timely and safe delivery of bulk chemicals" core process.

Part 4

Risk Management Structure

7 Risk Management Responsibilities

Risk Guidelines that include a framework of responsibilities will facilitate management of significant risks within the organisation

This chapter emphasises the need for a robust set of risk guidelines. For many organisations these risk guidelines will be established in writing. Sometimes, a risk management steering group will be appropriate. This group is likely to include the risk manager and representatives from internal audit, treasury and the strategy department. Normally, the finance director will chair the risk management steering group.

The risk guidelines will often include details of the risk management structure in place in the organisation. This structure can be described as the "Risk Architecture" for the organisation and it will set out risk management responsibilities. Also, details of the risk strategy and risk protocols will need to be included in the risk guidelines. The guidelines should also include details of the internal control responsibilities of managers.

The responsibilities related to risk management should be clearly set out in the guidelines with particular emphasis placed on the following:

1. Setting risk management strategy and policy;

2. Implementing risk management standards and procedures; and

3. Monitoring compliance with established standards

The end result will be a risk assurance management system or RAMS. The structure of the RAMS should be similar to the ISO9000 series of standards on quality assurance management systems, as outlined in chapter 9.

7.1. Risk Management Structure

The risk management structure in the organisation can be described as the risk architecture. The risk architecture sets out lines of communication for reporting on risk management issues and events. It is vital that the risk architecture reinforces the fact that the responsibility for managing risks remains with the owner of the key dependency that could be impacted by the risk. The primary responsibility for monitoring risk performance rests with the owner of the core process that is supported by that key dependency.

So that risk management can be fully embedded into the processes and activities of an organisation, a clear statement of risk management responsibilities is required. As part of the analysis of each priority significant risk, risk management responsibilities need to be clearly allocated in relation to the following aspects of managing that risk:

- development of risk strategy and standards;
- implementation of the agreed standards and procedures; and
- auditing compliance with the agreed standards

Figure 8 (overleaf) sets out a suitable structure for the risk architecture in a large organisation. The responsibilities of each group or committee are outlined in Figure 8, the expected flow of information is indicated. In many organisations, there will be no need for formalised committees concerned with risk management and internal control at departmental level. However, the duties and responsibilities assigned in Figure 8 to such a committee still need to be undertaken by individuals who work in the department.

The structure set out in Figure 8 is an integrated, and integrative, framework for the effective identification, evaluation, management, control and audit of the priority significant risks. The risk management structure is part of the risk assurance management system (RAMS) for the organisation.

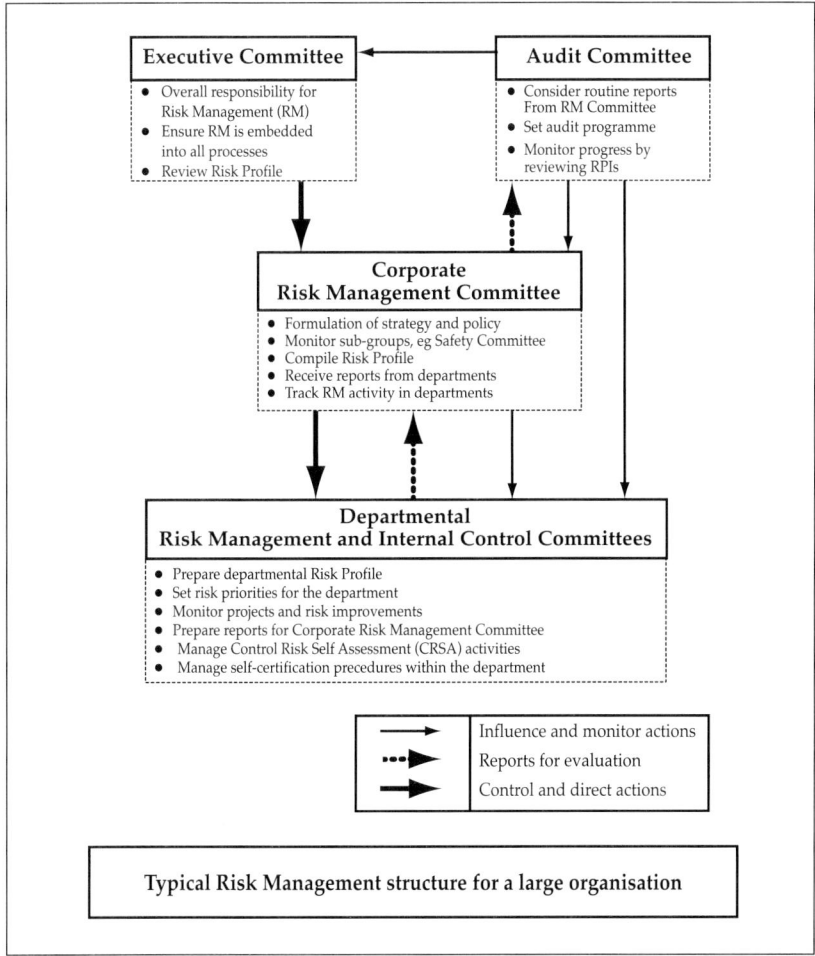

Figure 8: Risk Management Structure

7.1.1 Risk Management Policy

An illustration of suitable contents for the risk guidelines is set out in Table 5. These risk guidelines are discussed later in this chapter. Remember that the purpose of the risk guidelines is to describe the means by which a step change in the efficiency, competitiveness and leadership of the organisation will be achieved.

The risk management policy will form part of the risk guidelines for the organisation. The risk management policy should facilitate successful implementation of enhanced risk management in the organisation. The policy should confirm the protocols for undertaking the activities set out in the risk guidelines for the organisation. Specifically, the risk management policy should include details of at least the following:

- the board member responsible for the RAMS
- the language and perception of risk in the organisation
- the framework for identifying significant risks
- the role of the risk manager and internal auditors
- the terms of reference for the risk management group
- the risk management structure or architecture

7.1.2 Responsibility for Risk Management

Everybody working in or for the organisation will need to be made aware of his or her risk management responsibilities. There are many professional people in large organisations that have an understanding of risk and a substantial contribution to make to the successful management of the priority significant risks. Unfortunately, there is not always a common view of risk management or the issues that are important to the organisation.

The explicit statement of risk management responsibilities will assist with the ownership of risks and reinforce the ownership of risk management activities. These responsibilities should extend to a statement of the monitoring and reporting requirements placed on owners of the priority significant risks. The risk guidelines should also set out the procedures for regular review of the risk architecture, strategy and protocols (RASP) in place in the organisation.

The four headings of the FIRM Risk Scorecard represent financial, infrastructure, reputational and marketplace perspectives on risk. These are established areas of concern for organisations, so it should be easy to identify the responsibilities for reporting to the board on risks in these four areas. It is likely that the responsibilities will be allocated to board members, with information being reported to the appointed member by the following:

- financial   – reported by internal audit
- infrastructure – reported by operational management

- reputational – may not receive sufficient attention
- marketplace – reported by sales and marketing

Any confusion of responsibilities and reporting structure needs to be eliminated. There should be clear statements of responsibilities for the following aspects of the management of each priority significant risk:

- setting required risk performance standards
- implementing risk control procedures
- monitoring risk performance (RPIs)

This detailed set of responsibilities will ensure that the roles of risk owners, process owners, internal audit, risk manager and others are clearly defined and understood.

7.1.3   Risk Management Committee

In many cases, a Risk Management Committee (RMC) will need to be established. Most large organisations will already have an audit committee, chaired by a senior non-executive director. A key decision that needs to be taken is whether to extend the role of the audit committee to include all aspects of risk management or establish a separate risk management group chaired by an executive director.

RMC should be an executive group, rather than part of any existing non-executive audit committee. This is necessary because risks need to be managed in a pro-active manner as an executive responsibility. The existing audit committee is likely to treat the management of risk as a non-executive (reactive) auditing of compliance. Separation of executive responsibility for the management of risk from non-executive responsibility for auditing and review of compliance, will be consistent with good corporate governance principles.

Some organisations have established the RMC as a sub-committee of the audit committee. In many ways, this is the worst possible arrangement. This reporting structure could impair the work of the risk management group because of increased bureaucracy and an unhelpful emphasis on auditing and compliance, rather than pro-active management of risks. There are a number of decisions that need to be taken related to the way that the RMC and the audit committee should work together. These decisions are related to the scope and responsibilities of the two groups and the sharing of information. Figure 8 suggests a model, but this will not apply in all circumstances.

Membership of the RMC is another question that needs to be addressed. The fundamental decision to be taken in large organisations is whether the risk management committee should be a small senior executive group setting strategy and policy or whether it should be a knowledge sharing group with representation from each of the departments within the organisation. The answer will depend on the structure of the organisation and the intended role of the committee. In general, however, small committees are more effective.

The overall aim has to be to ensure a prioritised, validated and audited improvement in risk management standards in the organisation. The RMC and the audit committee should, therefore, operate in a way that provides mutual support. In most circumstances combining the two committees into a single group, or placing one committee as superior to the other is not going to be the best way forward.

Remember that, if a combined committee is established, then the combined committee will need to fulfil the role of an independent audit committee. Therefore, a non-executive director must chair the committee and non-executive directors must be in the majority. In these circumstances, it is unlikely that the committee will act as a forward looking, pro-active and dynamic group. In the absence of a separate RMC, it may be difficult for the combined committee to objectively receive the register of the priority significant risks for independent validation and sign off. Some of the members of the committee will have been directly involved in compiling the risk register.

7.1.4   Audit Committee

Figure 8 suggests a position and role for the separate audit committee. It receives reports from the RMC and from the internal and external auditors, so that it can report findings to the executive committee or board for evaluation and approval. The independent audit function is not shown in Figure 8 because its role should involve a review of the work and/or actions of any and all of the committees that are part of the risk architecture of the organisation.

The audit committee is concerned with internal control in the organisation. Internal control is described in the Turnbull report as "the whole system of controls, financial and otherwise, established in order to provide reasonable re-assurance of effective and efficient internal control and compliance with laws and regulations". This description implies that the role of the audit committee is to be responsible for monitoring and reviewing progress with improvements in internal control.

The audit committee should evaluate the effectiveness of the risk assurance management system (RAMS). This means that the audit committee will receive reports on the risk productivity indicators (RPIs) that have been allocated to the priority significant risks. These RPIs are the risk based key performance indicators. The audit committee will also need to consider at least the following:

- maintenance of the risk register
- appropriateness of the risk architecture
- terms of reference of the audit committee
- control self-certification arrangements

It is worth considering the role of the audit committee in relation to the requirements of the Turnbull report. The requirements in the report only apply to companies that are listed on the London Stock Exchange, although the principles set out in Turnbull appear to be gaining wider acceptance and application. One of the requirements of Turnbull is that companies without an internal audit department should review the need for such a function, on a routine basis.

Turnbull is an internal control report and it does not address all aspects of risk management. It requires companies to report on the effectiveness of the internal control framework within the organisation. The audit committee should take a wider view of risk management than just the scope of Turnbull and the committee should align itself with the broader scope of the risk guidelines.

The Turnbull report sets out a checklist of internal control questions, under the headings:

- control environment
- identification and evaluation of risks and control objectives
- information and communication
- control procedures
- monitoring and corrective action

Even if Turnbull does not apply to an organisation, it is still appropriate for the audit committee to ensure that it can fully respond to these questions, by ensuring that the necessary information is collected.

7.2   Risk Guidelines

The risk management guidelines define the risk architecture, strategy and protocols (RASP) for the organisation. The risk architecture is the structure for reporting and monitoring risks, as discussed in the previous section. The risk strategy is the overall view of risk in the organisation and the approach to individual priority significant risks, as necessary. The risk protocols are the various risk management systems and procedures that must be followed.

Table 5 outlines the likely contents of a typical set of risk guidelines. The risk guidelines describe the risk architecture and strategy, although the main focus of the risk guidelines is unlikely to be the risk protocols. The risk guidelines could form part of a more comprehensive risk management policy. The risk guidelines could be set out using the structure below:

- risk assessment

- risk control

- risk resourcing

- event management

- risk assurance

This structure is consistent with and reinforces the importance of the five activities involved in the risk management discipline. Each of these activities produces several outputs and the required outputs can be discussed in the risk guidelines. The requirements relating to these outputs can be described within the overall framework set out above.

The guidelines need not include a set of risk control standards, but should describe how risk control decisions will be taken, implemented and audited. In fact, the risk guidelines for a diverse group of companies cannot include physical control requirements and standards. Each division (or department) should set its own standards for risk control, including health and safety, fire safety, physical security, information security and environmental protection.

Embedded risk management will be achieved when the cycle of risk management activities is fully aligned with the planning cycle of the organisation. The risk guidelines should define the means by which embedded risk management is to be achieved in the organisation. The setting of strategy, standards and procedures needs to be undertaken within the framework of the risk guidelines. Typically, these guidelines will contain information on at least the following:

- financial and authorisation procedures

- insurance arrangements

- managers' control responsibilities

- project risk management

- incident reporting and investigation

- event planning

- physical risk control objectives and responsibilities

A primary purpose of the risk guidelines is to help managers understand the risk management framework of the organisation. This understanding will ensure that managers pay appropriate attention to risk implications when making decisions. The risk guidelines also provide practical guidance to managers on how to fulfil their risk management responsibilities.

The distribution of risk guidelines may be undertaken by way of a Risk Management Information System (RMIS) software package. The RMIS could be placed on the intranet of the organisation. The RMIS will also facilitate the collection and communication of risk information, including the reporting of CASE by local management, as they occur. Typically, the RMIS will include at least the following:

- risk management manual

- risk profile information

- details of the significant risks

- details of the core processes

- reaction plans and event management

- information on the total cost of risk

- claims and the loss experience

- insurance policy information
- risk improvement action plans
- corporate governance standards

Contents

1. Risk Management Framework
   - RM Policy and Strategy
   - RM Procedures and Protocols
   - Manager Control Responsibilities
   - Section of Staff Handbook related to Risk

2. Risk Assessment
   - Turnbull Procedures
   - Response to Significant Risks
   - Projects and CapEx Approvals
   - Procedures for Strategy and Budgets

3. Risk Control
   - Brand Management Guidelines
   - Health and Safety at Work
   - Environmental Protection
   - Contract Risk Management

4. Risk Resourcing
   - Opportunity Management
   - Resource Allocation
   - Insurance Programme
   - Captive Insurance Company

5. Event Management
   - Loss and Claims Management
   - Disaster and Recovery Planning
   - Cost Containment Procedures
   - Risk Management Record Keeping

6. Risk Assurance
   - Maintenance of Risk Register
   - Corporate RM Committee
   - Terms of Reference for Audit Committee
   - Control Self-Certification Arrangements

Typical contents for a set of Risk Management Guidelines

Table 5: Risk Management Guidelines

7.2.1   Risk Assessment

The selected methodology for undertaking risk assessments should be described in the risk guidelines. The risk assessment guidelines need to describe procedures to be applied to operations, projects and strategy. Typical requirements found in risk guidelines will include:

- procedures for the identification of potentially significant risks;

- means of identifying risk priorities;

- protocols for the approval of projects;

- standards for the risk assessment to be included with:

  — budget submissions;

  — capital expenditure (CapEx) applications; and

  — strategy plans

7.2.2   Risk Control

Control of risk in any organisation is the responsibility of local management. This will include the control of each priority significant risk at every stage of the life cycle of the risk. Local management must decide when it is necessary to introduce controls to reduce risk, when it is not worth the cost of introducing those controls and when the risk level has been reduced to an acceptable level.

The required standards of risk control should be described in the risk guidelines, to the extent that uniform standards need to be applied across the whole organisation. For risks that are specific to a department, the department itself should devise the risk control standards that will be applied. The risk guidelines need only establish control objectives and responsibilities – not specify detailed physical risk control standards.

Managers will have a wide range of control responsibilities. Historically these responsibilities will have been most clearly established in relation to internal financial control. As the risk management agenda has become more diverse, a developing requirement has been identified for managers' control responsibilities to be defined across this broader risk agenda.

Table 5 suggests some of the areas that need to be addressed in the risk guidelines. The level of detail to which an individual risk issue needs to be addressed in the organisation depends on the nature of the organisation and the variation between departments. The risk control issues that may need to be addressed include:

- brand management

- health and safety at work

- environmental protection

- contract risk management

- event planning

- data protection

- physical security

7.2.3 Risk Resourcing

The risk resourcing section of the guidelines should include reference to the methods for calculating values at risk in the organisation. This will include details of how a department should obtain authorisation for CapEx and projects, as appropriate. The attitude of the organisation to risk financing and resourcing will need to cover all types of core processes, key dependencies and all types of risks. Departments will need guidance on the methods to be used for calculating the values at risk, the total risk exposure and risk correlation. It is necessary to provide guidance on the total (or aggregate) risk exposure that the department is allowed to retain.

The important area of opportunity management should be covered, so that departments understand the values that can be put at risk when seeking to take advantage of perceived opportunities. Allocation of resources to projects and enhancements should also be covered. The extent of insurance that the organisation intends to buy in respect of hazard risks should be described and justified.

7.2.4 Event Management

Reaction planning and event management are vitally important aspects of successfully managing risks, especially in relation to projects and enhancements. The required standards of event management should be described in the risk guidelines. For hazard risks, the risk guidelines should confirm the requirement that departments must produce necessary business continuity plans.

Event planning is well established in relation to hazard risks, but the equivalent planning activities for control risks and to a greater extent opportunity risks are not as well developed. Control risk event management has received attention in most large organisations, in that internal audit plans (to be activated in the event of a major failing of controls) will usually have been produced.

For opportunity risks, there is a temptation to think about how good it would be to have the "problems of success". There is a belief that these problems can be easily managed, although this is not always true. Many positive circumstances, actions, situations and events (CASE) can be anticipated and a well managed organisation will seek to create conditions where opportunity risks are more likely to materialise. Plans to cope with these positive CASE and ensure maximum benefit from opportunity risks should be devised by the organisation and/or by each department.

7.2.5 Risk Assurance

Risk monitoring and communications are very important aspects of ensuring adequate management of risks. Also, structured reviews of risk performance and broader risk management arrangements are vital. The arrangements for risk monitoring and risk review together form the risk assurance activity and these arrangements should be explained in the risk guidelines. Protocols need to be established for monitoring opportunity risks. There needs to be complete alignment of the risk management structure and activities with other management activities in the organisation.

The role of the audit committee has already been discussed and the distinction between risk monitoring as a routine management activity and risk review as a more formal audit activity has been outlined. The role of the audit committee is mainly in the context of risk review. The role of the audit committee in respect of auditing and review needs to be defined in this section of the risk guidelines.

The risk guidelines should be structured to ensure that there is compatibility between the different approaches to risk management within the organisation. Generally, managers will need information for decision making and/or mechanisms for recording risk data. Implementation of the risk management structure and the risk guidelines, together with the possible introduction of a RMIS, should provide the assurance that the requirements of the board with respect to risk management are satisfied.

7.3   Ownership of Risk

Ownership of core processes, key dependencies and risks is important, because it enables the risk management and audit committees to monitor actions and responsibilities. This ownership is important for all risks, although the audit committee will only monitor the priority significant risks.

Ownership of the core processes is necessary in an organisation. Each core process in the organisation should be the explicit responsibility of a board member. This structure of ownership leads to a position where the owner of a key dependency is responsible for managing the risks that could impact that key dependency. The owner of the core process is then responsible for monitoring the management of the key dependencies and associated risks. The owner of the core process will monitor management of the risks by reference to the allocated risk productivity indicators (RPIs).

The information on ownership of each priority significant risk and ownership of each core process should be included in the risk register. There will be an owner of each core process with responsibility for delegating ownership of each key dependency and the risks that could impact that key dependency. The owner of each key dependency will normally be the person with ownership of the associated risks. That person will also have responsibility for reporting any CASE relevant to the risks, as well as reporting on performance against the allocated RPIs.

Note that the actions of the risk manager, risk management committee, audit committee, internal auditors and others should not reduce local ownership of core processes and key dependencies. Managers must see ownership of risks as integral to the management of core processes and key dependencies, not as a separate issue that is the responsibility of specialist professional risk management practitioners.

Summary and Review of Chapter 7

Section 1 explores many of the issues associated with establishing a suitable risk management structure or architecture. The fundamental objective to be achieved is that the risk management structure is aligned with business imperatives, business strategy and budget formulation. The structure should ensure that risk management is aligned (and embedded) with management of the core processes.

It is important that the structure is clearly set out, so that interested parties become fully aware of their responsibilities. Section 1 made it clear that the establishment of clear lines of communication is fundamentally important. This will ensure that the protocols for managing risks are clearly understood.

Section 2 suggests contents for the "Risk Guidelines". The risk guidelines provide information on how people within the organisation should fulfil their risk management responsibilities. The guidelines and the risk management policy can be structured to reflect the five activities that make up the risk management discipline.

Organisations need to decide whether written risk guidelines are necessary. If a written risk management manual is required, then the managers' control responsibilities should be clearly stated in the manual. One of the main benefits of producing written guidelines is that the required risk management input into the budgeting and strategy aspects of managing the organisation can be explicitly stated.

The main message of the chapter is that a clear framework, with explicitly stated responsibilities, is required if risks are to be robustly managed. Ownership of the risks is the most important benefit that will be achieved. The best structure for risk management guidelines is based on the five activities involved in the risk management discipline. Case Study 7 consolidates the key messages outlined in this chapter.

Case Study 7: Magazine Publisher – (Part 2)

There are many risks facing a publisher and there is a need to co-ordinate the risk management effort. This case study is about the need for appropriate risk guidelines setting out the risk architecture, strategy and protocols (RASP) for an organisation. It is also about the need to have clearly established risk protocols and procedures.

Barbican Publishing Limited faces risks associated with the collection of information, writing of articles, production and distribution of magazines etc. It is likely that a key area of risk will be libel and slander. The core process at risk is "provision of high quality and accurate journalism"

The risk control standards for libel and slander will depend on the level of risk exposure and the context that gives rise to libel and slander risks. It may vary from title to title within Barbican Publishing, but it would be broadly in accordance with the following:

- all journalists given libel and slander training

- specific review procedures for certain titles

- legal evaluation of individual high risk articles

Barbican Publishing will need to decide what it is seeking to achieve in the area of libel and slander (strategy), the systems and procedures it will put in place to monitor performance (protocols) and the means for reporting and communication (architecture). The risk guidelines will set out the:

- risk assessment protocols;

- risk control objectives;

- risk resourcing procedures;

- event management requirements; and

- risk assurance systems

The framework (or risk architecture) set up to achieve adequate management of risks should also be presented. It will be for the individual titles in the group to operate within the framework.

Barbican Publishing needs to establish detailed risk guidelines. These risk guidelines will be produced using the expertise within the organisation and drawing on external support, as necessary. Although not a specialist in libel and slander, the risk manager will be able to assist with the establishment of the risk architecture, strategy and protocols (RASP) for managing this specialist area of risk. The in-house source of expertise relevant to this risk is likely to be in the legal department.

8 Risk and the Risk Manager

Risk Manager must develop the role in order to become the Guardian of the Risk Architecture, Strategy and Protocols (GRASP)

This chapter considers the changing role and responsibilities of the risk manager. Historically, the title risk manager has been applied to the person responsible for the purchase of insurance. Recently, the role of the risk manager has extended to include risk control and decisions on the level of retention of insurable risks within the organisation. As the role of the risk manager has extended, it has become obvious that one individual is not able to provide expertise in all areas of risk, even all those areas within hazard risk.

If a wider involvement and influence for the risk manager is to be successful, then the "Barriers and Actions" to achieving improved management of risk will need to be evaluated and overcome. The barriers and actions will be unique to an organisation. The risk manager will have to be the champion of the development and implementation of the risk assurance management system (RAMS). The risk manager will also need to be able to explain the contribution that risk management can make to the achievement of the mission and explain the benefits of full implementation of risk productivity.

Against this background, there is clearly a need to establish a redefined role for the risk manager. This chapter suggests that the role should be "Guardian of the Risk Architecture, Strategy and Protocols" or GRASP. It is a strange contradiction that, at the same time as the importance of risk management is increasing, the role of the risk manager is becoming less well defined. As GRASP, the new risk manager should promote risk management, whilst retaining a key co-ordination and facilitation role.

8.1. Role of the Risk Manager

Organisations need a facilitator and co-ordinator for their risk management efforts. There is a need to redefine the role of the risk manager. The approach suggested in this book is that the risk manager should become the guardian of the risk architecture, strategy and protocols. (GRASP). At the same time, a risk assurance management system (RAMS) will need to be introduced under the sponsorship of a board director. The risk architecture strategy and protocols (RASP) will be the day to day implementation structure of the RAMS. In summary, implementation of the RASP together with the actions taken to achieve risk productivity will form the RAMS. The steps to achieving risk productivity are discussed in chapter 9.

It is the function of the risk manager and the RASP to be creative. The RASP should not be something that the risk manager has created. Unfortunately, most insurance risk managers start from a weak position. Generally, the insurance risk manager, and the discipline of risk management, has not been involved in business decisions. The problems of low seniority, limited business experience and a staid role must be overcome before the risk manager, and risk management, can make a full contribution to the achievement of the corporate mission.

Historically, the risk manager has not been involved in the strategic management and development of the organisation. Now that the importance of risk management is expanding, it is becoming obvious that the insurance risk manager does not currently have the experience to be able to make a full contribution. Typically, risk managers still do not have the business experience or the knowledge of strategic issues in the organisation to be able to facilitate discussions and make a valued contribution.

This chapter looks at the historical role of the risk manager and suggests how the role can be developed in future. Despite the restricted historical role of risk managers, they are still the best suited individuals to facilitate the integrative risk management approach. After all, no other person in the organisation will have the breadth of practical experience of risk assessment that the risk manager can offer.

8.1.1 Historical Role of the Risk Manager

Risk management professionals need to be confident in the contribution that they have made in the past and can make in the future. There is no single established reporting position in the structure of an organisation for the risk manager. At present, risk managers can be found who report to human resources, the finance director or the company secretary. Sometimes, the risk manager will report to the corporate treasurer and occasionally, the chief executive officer (CEO).

Some sectors of industry have well developed risk management functions. For example, in the finance and energy sectors, the risk manager, as chief risk officer (CRO), is a board member and a direct report to the CEO. The title and seniority of CRO tends to be almost exclusively restricted to these sectors at present.

The typical historical role of the risk manager has been to undertake tasks, as follows:

1. Establish the risk management strategy for protecting company property and people

2. Co-ordinate the company insurance programme through the captive insurance company

3. Work with the manager of the captive to maximise the contribution made by the captive insurance company

4. Maintain key insurer relationships, monitor service providers and ensure cost effective placement of insurance contracts

5. Measure and monitor cost of risk performance of the group and individual group companies

6. Ensure safe keeping and adequate retention of all insurance contracts and agreements

7. Supervise the co-ordination of service provider activities and place the group and global insurances

8. Co-ordinate the property survey programme, risk management procedures and any premium discount incentive schemes

Historically, the risk manager has been involved in assessing the overall risk policy with endorsement from the board. Decisions on insurance risk management issues and the provision of statistical analysis of insurance losses have been part of these historical responsibilities. The risk manager has also been required to review the effectiveness of implementation of risk management policy and strategy.

An important part of the historical responsibilities has been to produce reports on risk management initiatives and also reports on loss statistics. The risk manager has also been required to facilitate discussion across the businesses and facilitate the sharing of expertise. Yet, at the same time, the traditional risk manager has lacked the business skills to make a full contribution to broader management issues.

Until recently, large organisations have employed a risk manager and a large risk management department. The risk manager would have come from an insurance background. The size of the department was fully justified, on the basis that the historical role of the risk manager was to look after hazard risks and hazard management, a major component of hazard management is the purchase of insurance.

Many risk managers continue to fulfil the role described above. Indeed, the role of insurance manager is still necessary. Reviewing the historical role of the risk manager helps focus on the need for change and the scope for an enhanced role for the risk manager, in the future. In short, an integrative model is required to ensure that the contribution that can be made by risk management is not lost to the organisation. The risk manager will have a vitally important role to play in the development and implementation of this integrative model. There is no need for most organisations to out-source risk management and Turnbull compliance. The role of the risk manager can be developed to co-ordinate this work.

The insurance risk manager needs to evaluate the current status of risk management. Increases in insurance rates and a more sophisticated approach to risk financing have reduced the amount of insurance purchased by large organisations. Less insurance purchased, means a reduced premium spend and a lower budget for the risk management department. The status of the insurance risk manager has reduced as a result. The end result has been that many risk managers now report to the corporate treasurer, instead of being a direct report to the group finance director.

8.1.2   Developing Role of the Risk Manager

There is a need for a risk management facilitator and co-ordinator in most large organisations. This will enable the organisation to apply risk management tools and techniques to a wider range of issues. It is no longer sensible to be limited by historical divisions between risk practitioners. The risk manager should develop the role and become the guardian of the risk architecture, strategy and protocols (GRASP).

Risks have historically been divided into insurable and non-insurable or pure and speculative risks. These are artificial divisions between types of risks. There is a need to identify the risks that could impact the key dependencies, core processes, corporate objectives and, ultimately, the mission of the organisation. Risk management has emerged as a major management initiative because of the rapidly changing business environment. Accordingly, the discipline of risk management will inevitably have an increasingly important contribution to make to the improved management and corporate governance of organisations into the future.

Now that control management has been given a higher profile, with the publication the Turnbull report, recently appointed risk managers may come from an accountancy background as well as from an insurance background. However, the new accountancy risk manager is no better equipped to look after the broad risk management agenda than is the insurance risk manager.

If risk management is to accept the new challenge and to expand into opportunity management, a broader set of skills is required. Risk managers need to understand the relationships within business activities and core processes. In the role of guardian of the risk architecture, strategy and protocols (GRASP), the risk manager will need to be an enthusiastic champion for embedding risk management into core processes and the management of key dependencies.

In summary, the risk manager will be responsible for the corporate learning that has to take place so that the organisation can understand what is to be gained from risk management. As GRASP, the risk manager will be responsible for developing the strategy, systems and procedures by which the required outcomes are to be achieved. Also, the development of the risk protocols that need to be implemented will be the responsibility of the GRASP.

The requirement is to develop and communicate the risk policy and then provide adequate training and information to be able to demonstrate that enhanced corporate performance and corporate governance can be achieved. The board sponsor of the risk productivity initiative will have a wider view than simply the systems and procedures that need to be introduced. The nominated board member will have ownership of the risk assurance management system (RAMS). In most cases, it will be appropriate for the risk manager to report to that board member.

8.1.3   Chief Risk Officer

Perhaps the title "Risk Manager" has too many historical connections for it to be used as an appropriate description of what is now required. If risks are to be managed within the business and if risks are to be evaluated in terms of the impact on core business processes and key dependencies, then a new set of skills is necessary. There is a need to find a new title and re-define the role of risk management at the same time. For example, the need for a chief risk officer (CRO) and the relationship between the insurance risk manager and head of internal audit are just two issues that need to be agreed on.

Many organisations in the finance and energy sectors have identified the benefits of bringing the management of credit, operational and market risks together. These categories of risk are related to the financial, infrastructure and marketplace headings of the FIRM Risk Scorecard. Credit risk is related to internal financial control, operational risks are associated with infrastructure issues and market risk is clearly associated with the marketplace. It is interesting to note that, although the creation of the CRO role is exciting, it does not embrace the full scope of the FIRM Risk Scorecard. Responsibility for the management and co-ordination of reputational risks is generally omitted.

In the finance sector, risk management has been an established function, separate from the purchase of insurance. The development of the role of chief risk officer reflects this fact. For almost all other organisations, risk management will remain a management initiative and, therefore, it will not be appropriate to appoint a new member of the board called the CRO. In any case, most chief executive officers recognise that the role and responsibilities of the CRO are, in fact, CEO responsibilities that should not be delegated to another board member.

The introduction of the job title chief risk officer (CRO) is not universal, but it is becoming common in the specialist finance and energy sectors. Guardian of the risk architecture, strategy and protocols (GRASP) is a superior description of the role that must be fulfilled in order to successfully deliver the benefits of integrative risk management, described in this book as risk productivity. Although the title CRO may not be universally recognised, it is even less likely that the title GRASP will become commonly used. Nevertheless, the title is worth exploring in more detail, in the following sections.

8.2.   Guardian of the RASP

The proposed role for the risk manager is to become Guardian of the Risk Architecture, Strategy and Protocols (GRASP) for the organisation. The risk architecture, strategy and protocols have the following meanings, as set out in Appendix A:

- the risk architecture is the risk management arrangements, including details of committees, reporting structures and responsibilities

- the risk strategy is the statement of what the organisation is seeking to achieve with respect to the management of risks

- the risk protocols set out how the strategy is implemented, including details of how risk management activities are undertaken

The contribution that risk management can make to the fulfilment of the mission for the organisation is increasingly understood. To ensure that risk management delivers all of the benefits that are anticipated, a co-ordinator is required. The co-ordinator will be the risk manager, perhaps using a new title. The new title for the risk manager should reflect what is expected of the new risk manager.

Guardian of the risk architecture, strategy and protocols (GRASP) may not be an elegant title, but it is very descriptive of the nature and scope of the task. The new risk manager is required to facilitate the activities involved in the risk management discipline. The challenge for the risk manager is to demonstrate the benefits of applying risk management tools and techniques to the management of the full range of risks, as set out in the FIRM Risk Scorecard for the organisation.

Clearly, the GRASP cannot have first hand experience in all of these risk areas. Also, it will not be the responsibility of the GRASP to be accountable for the successful implementation of all risk management standards. The role of the risk manager rests in the area of strategy formulation and ensuring that adequate risk procedures and protocols are in place and fully implemented.

Remember that the GRASP cannot be directly responsible for the day-to-day management of risks. In any event, organisations with dedicated specialist functions would not wish the risk manager to fulfil that responsibility. The owner of a risk is likely to be the person with responsibility for managing the key dependency that could be impacted by that risk. The owner of the core process that is supported by that key dependency will be responsible for monitoring all of the risks that could impact all of the key dependencies supporting that core process.

8.2.1   Risk Architecture

Risk architecture is composed of risk management arrangements, including details of committees, reporting structures and the risk management responsibilities. The architecture is the "who" and "when" of the risk management. This is usually represented as a reporting structure with associated arrangements and, when necessary, the committee structure for risk management. Figure 8 in chapter 7 is an example of the risk architecture for a large organisation.

Allocating responsibilities within the risk architecture and showing that the whole system works as an integrated, and integrative, whole is the major contribution that can be made by the GRASP. However, it is impossible for one individual, or even a small department, to have responsibility for implementing all of the risk management standards and procedures in respect of all priority significant risks.

The risk manager will support the risk architecture in the role of GRASP. As guardian, the risk manager will direct and advise the board on the application of the risk management discipline throughout the organisation. The risk manager will specifically report on certain risks and ensure that adequate attention is paid to risk management within projects. The risk manager will seek to facilitate the integration of risk management with the planning, control and monitoring of the core processes in the organisation.

The risk architecture should require that risk management considerations play an important part in making major decisions. Implementing the risk architecture should not be a response to specific risks, but rather it should describe the way in which the organisation allocates responsibilities for the management of risks. Organisations should be careful to ensure that what is planned as strategic or integrative risk management does not degenerate into, or revert to, operational risk response.

There are dangers in establishing an independent risk management architecture, structure and sets of protocols. The main danger is that risk management comes to be seen as a separate activity, rather than embedded into core processes. The main imperative for the risk architecture is that it should eliminate the impression that risk management is a separate management activity carried out remote from the day-to-day management of core processes and key dependencies.

8.2.2   Risk Strategy

Risk Strategy is the statement of what the organisation is seeking to achieve in risk management. The strategy is the "why" and "what" of risk management and sets out what has to be done. The risk strategy will ensure the continuity of risk management input into decision making activities, so that risk management ceases to be a static, reactive and detached activity.

Effective risk management drives the achievement of the mission and corporate objectives of the organisation. Effective risk management equates exactly with successful management of the organisation. It is worth reflecting this fact in the risk strategy. There has to be a relationship between risk strategy and the risk capacity of the organisation, this should be acknowledged in the stated risk strategy. The mechanisms for identification of the risk capacity of the organisation and the calculation of the actual risk exposure are important aspects of the risk management strategy.

It is important for the strategy to be as specific as possible with respect to the desire of the organisation to quantify individual values at risk and determine the overall risk exposure of the organisation. The risk capacity needs to be established, together with the approach to dealing with risks that are not correlated and, therefore, considered unlikely to materialise at the same time, or during the period under consideration.

The risk strategy must not become static and detached from the dynamic management of the organisation. The risk strategy can be outlined in the risk management policy, but it should be written in a flexible way that ensures that it will remain proactive and relevant to changing circumstances.

8.2.3 Risk Protocols

Risk Protocols set out how the strategy is to be implemented, including details of how risk management activities will be undertaken. The risk protocols are the "where" and "how" of risk management and set out how the strategy will be achieved. The contribution that risk management is expected to make should be defined by the risk protocols. In many ways, this is the most important section of the risk guidelines. The risk protocols will be the practical procedures and systems by which the risk strategy is implemented. Remember that the risk strategy will be communicated through the risk architecture and implemented via the risk protocols.

Risk protocols need to be established in relation to the requirement to undertake risk assessments as part of business strategy formulation, and as part of budgeting activities. The means by which risk management is embedded into project management will need to be specified in the risk protocols. These protocols will also include internal audit arrangements, risk audit returns, arrangements for risk workshops and other company arrangements for control self-certification and/or control risk self assessment (CRSA). The risk protocols are the means of ensuring that the risk management activities are fully linked to the core processes of the organisation.

Chapter 7 sets out a suggested structure for the risk guidelines. The guidelines will describe the risk protocols that are in place in the organisation. Clearly, the risk protocols will need to be dynamic and develop with time. In accordance with the requirements of the risk assurance management system (RAMS), there will be a need to routinely review the risk protocols.

8.3 Barriers to Implementation

It is important that the risk manager identifies the barriers to the implementation of risk productivity in some detail. There are many factors that will influence the effectiveness of the risk productivity approach and the success of the risk manager. These factors include:

- senior management influence within departments
- external influences, including corporate governance
- nature of the business, its products and culture
- corporate attitudes, including previous RM experiences
- origins of the risk management department

145

Identification of the barriers, as set out in Table 6, leads to the ability to put in place actions to overcome the barriers. Analysis of these barriers within the context of the specific organisation will lead to the identification of the best options to ensure that risk management delivers the optimum benefits. Different specific actions may be required in different organisations, but Table 6 provides outline

	Barrier	Action
1.	Lack of understanding of risk management and belief that it will suppress entrepreneurship	Establish a shared understanding, common expectations and a consistent language of risk in the organisation
2.	Lack of support and commitment from senior management	Identify a sponsor on the main board of the organisation and confirm shared and common priorities
3.	Seen as just another initiative, so relevance and importance not accepted	Agree a strategy that sets out the anticipated outcomes and confirms the nature of the anticipated benefits
4.	Benefits not perceived as being significant	Complete a realistic analysis of what can be achieved and the impact on the mission of the organisation
5.	Not seen as a core part of business activity and too time consuming	Align effort with core processes and achievement of the mission of the organisation
6.	Approach too complicated and over-analytical (risk overkill)	Establish appropriate level of sophistication for risk management framework and the undertaking of risk assessments
7.	Responsibilities unclear and need for external consultants unclear	Establish agreed risk architecture with clear roles and accepted risk responsibilities
8.	Risks separated from where they arose and should be managed	Include risk management in job descriptions to ensure that risks are managed within the context that gave rise to the risks
9.	Risk management seen as static activity not appropriate for a dynamic organisation	Align risk management effort with the mission of the organisation and with the business decision making activities
10.	Risk management too expansive and seeking to take over all aspects of the company	Be realistic. Do not claim that **all** of the business activities within the organisation are risk management by another name

> **There are many barriers to the introduction of Risk Productivity**

Table 6: Implementation Barriers and Actions

guidance on how to overcome the barriers to the implementation of risk productivity.

As listed in Table 6, there are many barriers to the implementation of a successful risk management initiative. These include the fact that successful risk management requires the commitment of all parties and implementation will only be as good as the least committed member of a department. Improved management of risks will take time to achieve and risk productivity may initially be seen as negative and bureaucratic.

There is no single action that will ensure adequate implementation and no single timeframe by which implementation will be fully achieved. Nevertheless, chapter 10 does offer some thoughts on the timeframe for implementation of the risk productivity approach. As suggested in chapter 10, full implementation of all stages of the approach may take between 2 and 5 years.

Summary and Review of Chapter 8

Section 1 discussed the changed and expanded role of the risk manager. It is unrealistic to expect the risk manager to be an expert in all aspects of risk. Despite years of experience that can be brought to bear on specific classes of risk, the risk agenda is now too wide to be within the expertise of one individual. The contribution to be made by the risk manager, in future, will be as guardian of the risk architecture, strategy and protocols (GRASP).

The duties and responsibilities associated with the management of risks should be described in the risk management policy. This risk management policy will describe the risk management obligations and duties of all people involved in and with the organisation.

Section 2 suggested that as guardian of the risk architecture, strategy and protocols (GRASP), the risk manager would have a range of responsibilities. Risk strategy is the description of what needs to be achieved with respect to risk. The risk protocols are the systems and procedures by which the strategy is fulfilled and the risk architecture is the structure, including means of communication, designed to ensure that the risk strategy is being delivered.

Establishing the context within which risks will be managed is a vital prerequisite to the successful management of the risks. The final details of the risk architecture, strategy and protocols (RASP) can only be finalised when the context within which the risks arise has been fully analysed. However, it should not be set up as a part of the response to any specific risk, because the RASP needs to reflect the context and nature of the portfolio of priority significant risks. The RASP should also reflect the culture of the organisation and the nature of the core processes that exist within the organisation.

The main message from this chapter is that there is a need for the role of the risk manager to develop and become guardian of the risk architecture, strategy and protocols. In this role, the risk manager will need to identify, analyse and then overcome many barriers to the implementation of integrative risk management in the organisation. Case Study 8 consolidates the key messages outlined in this chapter.

Case Study 8: Chemical Road Tankers – (Part 2)

Holborn Chemical Transport Limited (HCT) has a number of existing core processes. HCT now wishes to expand its activities by undertaking a new venture. Risk management tools and techniques will be applied to this new venture. Following a strategic review, HCT has set up the strategic core process "expand chemical management services into customer premises".

The challenge for the risk manager is to ensure that the risk guidelines are developed (if necessary) and then applied to the proposed business development. This will bring benefits to the strategic plans for the introduction of the proposed new customer services. The risk manager has been invited to the planning meetings. The questions that the risk manager needs to put to the first meeting are intended to set the risk management agenda for the development of the proposed new services.

The discussion at the first meeting should concentrate on the following three risk management questions:

1. What is the risk management strategy during the development of the proposed services? What is HCT seeking to achieve in terms of managing the risks to this core process?

2. What protocols will be devised and implemented to undertake the five risk management activities? How will HCT implement the desired risk strategy?

3. What risk architecture should be established for the project and how does this relate to the existing risk architecture? How will HCT monitor successful management of risks?

The role and job description of the risk manager or guardian of the risk architecture, strategy and protocols (GRASP) has provided the structure for the risk management input into the development of the new core process. Questions can now be asked about the priority significant risks that could impact the key dependencies that will support this new core process.

Discussions can take place about the values put at risk by the priority significant risks facing this new core process. Calculation of the values at risk, leading to awareness of the total risk exposure will be facilitated by the GRASP. The risk exposure, adjusted for correlation between risks, can then be determined and compared with the risk capacity. Allocation of risk capacity can then occur, finally the risk productivity indicators (RPIs) can be allocated.

Part 5

Summary and Review

9

Achieving Risk Productivity

Risk Productivity Indicators (RPIs) provide the mechanism for aligning risk management activities with the corporate mission

This chapter sets out the steps to achieving "Risk Productivity". The steps include consideration of the mission statement and analysis of corporate objectives and stakeholder expectations. Core processes deliver stakeholder expectations and require the support of key dependencies. Analysis of the key dependencies leads to the identification and analysis of the priority significant risks. As the register of the priority significant risks is compiled, decisions can be made about the measurements that will be applied to the monitoring of these risks. These risk-based measurements are labelled risk productivity indicators or RPIs.

There is also some further consideration in this chapter of RPIs and the allocation of risk capacity to hazard risks, control risks and opportunity risks. The allocation of risk capacity under the four headings of the FIRM Risk Scorecard is also considered. The need for an organisation to confirm that the actual risk exposure does not exceed the allotted risk capacity is also addressed. The risk assurance management system or RAMS is the overall system that exists in the organisation. Implementation of the risk architecture, strategy and protocols (RASP) together with the actions taken to achieve risk productivity, represent the risk assurance management system (RAMS) for the organisation.

Risk productivity indicators (RPIs) provide the mechanism for aligning risk management activities with the corporate mission. These indicators can be designed to monitor the upside contribution of opportunity risks, as well as monitoring management of control risks and hazard risks.

9.1.   Twelve Steps to Risk Productivity

This section sets out the methodology that defines the way in which risk productivity is achieved. The basis of achieving risk productivity is the design and implementation of the risk assurance management system (RAMS). The approach builds on the ideas and concepts outlined in the previous chapters. The approach is illustrated in the consolidated case study in Appendix B.

Risk productivity is the concept that defines the contribution that can be made by risk management to the achievement of the mission of the organisation. The organisation should ensure that a cost effective return is achieved and full use is made of the risk capacity of the organisation. All organisations should utilise risk capacity to the full and measure the benefits to the organisation of using its full risk capacity, by means of appropriate risk productivity indicators (RPIs).

Figure 9 sets out the twelve steps to achieving risk productivity. Figure 9 is the basis of an overall approach and it is sufficiently well developed to form the basis of a risk assurance management system (RAMS), as discussed later in this chapter. Many of the actions and activities described in Figure 9 happen already in most organisations. The introduction of risk productivity is more likely to be successful, if risk management protocols are built on the existing protocols of the organisation. Remember that implementation of the RASP together with the actions taken to achieve risk productivity will form the RAMS.

The twelve steps are grouped into four risk management phases. The characteristics of each of these phases are more fully explored in chapter 10. They are presented as the four boxes in Figure 9, as follows:

1. Organising for Risk Management –   Integrative phase

2. Evaluating the Risk Environment –   Holistic phase

3. Aligning the Significant Risks   –   Alignment phase

4. Embedding Appropriate Actions   –   Embedding phase

Risk productivity is a means of focusing on risks and ensuring that the attention of managers is directed towards making full use of the risk capacity of the organisation. What is really important is that the core processes that deliver stakeholder expectations are robust. The risks that could impact the key dependencies that support these core processes must be properly analysed and managed.

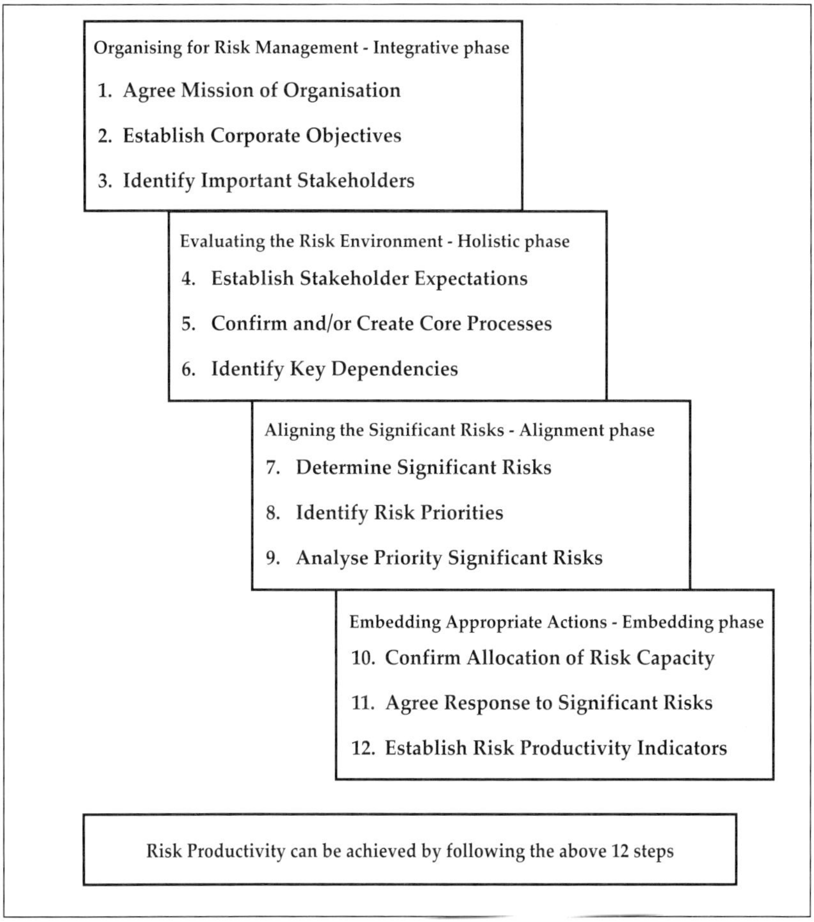

Organising for Risk Management - Integrative phase

1. Agree Mission of Organisation

2. Establish Corporate Objectives

3. Identify Important Stakeholders

Evaluating the Risk Environment - Holistic phase

4. Establish Stakeholder Expectations

5. Confirm and/or Create Core Processes

6. Identify Key Dependencies

Aligning the Significant Risks - Alignment phase

7. Determine Significant Risks

8. Identify Risk Priorities

9. Analyse Priority Significant Risks

Embedding Appropriate Actions - Embedding phase

10. Confirm Allocation of Risk Capacity

11. Agree Response to Significant Risks

12. Establish Risk Productivity Indicators

Risk Productivity can be achieved by following the above 12 steps

Figure 9: Achieving Risk Productivity

9.1.1   Mission of Organisation

Even if an organisation does not have clearly defined corporate objectives, there will always be a reason for the organisation to exist. This "reason to exist" helps to develop and define the mission of the organisation. That mission may be as simple as "to be the biggest food retailer in the country".

The mission sets out what the organisation is seeking to achieve at a high level. For the sake of example, consider the Aldgate Theatre mentioned in case studies 2 and 4. The mission for the Aldgate Theatre is: "to become the leading presenter of low budget, popular entertainment productions in the country".

9.1.2   Corporate Objectives

A consideration of the corporate objectives is important because they are the means by which the mission is to be achieved. Also, the most commonly used definition of risk refers to risks as "anything that can impact achievement of corporate objectives". Some organisations operate a system of ensuring that objectives are structured throughout the organisation. This approach ensures that the departmental objectives are established within the context of the corporate objectives. A more consistent approach to setting corporate objectives, as well as better structured departmental and corporate objectives are the benefits of this approach.

The corporate objectives establish the targets or plans that must be fulfilled if the mission is to be achieved. However, most organisations tend to quote objectives as internal, annual, change objectives, rather than as a full statement of the short term, medium term and long term aims of the organisation. A full statement of objectives would set out the operational (or efficiency), change (or competition) and strategic (or leadership), objectives of the organisation.

The setting of corporate objectives is the output from the internal evaluation stage of the business cycle that is set out in Figure 5 in chapter 4. The corporate objectives could be presented using the framework of the FIRM Risk Scorecard. This will result in the identification of financial, infrastructure, reputational and marketplace (FIRM) objectives. The following are examples of some of the likely FIRM objectives for the Aldgate Theatre.

Financial

The overall financial requirement is "to ensure successful management of money received by the theatre".

Financial objectives include:

- to ensure that adequate financial controls are in place to deliver a profit margin of 20% of gross income; and

- to ensure that CapEx approvals are rigorous and include a detailed risk assessment

Infrastructure

The overall infrastructure requirement is "to achieve optimal level of efficiency and achieve desired state of NUDE"

Infrastructure objectives include:

- to ensure that customer enquiries are handled within 7 days and complaints do not exceed 1 in 50,000 guests; and

- to ensure efficient theatre booking and confirmation arrangements

Reputational

The overall reputational requirement is "to ensure required level of respect for the theatre, leading to strong customer desire to attend shows"

Reputational objectives include:

- to ensure that at least 400 ticket sales enquiries are received per day; and

- to ensure that there is substantial customer recognition of the theatre name

Marketplace

The overall marketplace requirement is "to ensure the required level of customer retention and expenditure"

Marketplace objectives include:

- to achieve an average additional guest spend of £10 per visit to the theatre; and

- to ensure that suppliers and sponsors remain happy with the level of customer spend in the in-house franchise operations

Note that objectives are necessary, but they present a high level strategic view of the organisation that makes it difficult to successfully identify and attach risks to objectives. This difficulty remains, even when objectives are written as practical and structured statements. However, objectives are often written as somewhat intangible and vague goals. The analysis of the organisation, in this case the Aldgate Theatre, needs to continue, so that a more satisfactory attachment point for risks can be identified.

9.1.3 Stakeholders

All organisations have stakeholders. The stakeholders may be individuals, groups and/or other organisations. Analysis of the stakeholders of the organisation provides an approach that will lead to the successful identification and rigorous management of risks.

Some stakeholders may be unwanted. Indeed, most organisations will have stakeholders that they do not want. For the Aldgate Theatre, the local residents association (as an example) may lobby against expansion plans and may, therefore be unwanted stakeholders. For most organisations, stakeholders will include at least the following:

- customers
- staff
- financiers and shareholders
- sponsors and suppliers
- pressure groups
- Government

Stakeholders have expectations that should be reflected in the mission statement and in the corporate objectives. However, a more detailed evaluation of stakeholder expectations will help to extend the range of corporate activities covered. This will also ensure that the core processes within the organisation are better focused on the main requirements of the stakeholders.

Undertaking steps 1, 2 and 3 completes the
"organising for risk management"
or the integrative phase of risk productivity

9.1.4   Stakeholder Expectations

Stakeholders have expectations of the organisation. A stakeholder expectation is a requirement that the stakeholder places on the organisation. Stakeholders are identified in step 3 so that their expectations of the organisation can be evaluated.

Different stakeholders may have expectations that are contradictory or even mutually exclusive in terms of the demands placed on the organisation. Also, the unwanted stakeholders will have expectations that cannot be ignored. The organisation will often be obligated to respond to the expectations of these unwanted stakeholders. The identification of stakeholder expectations is the output from the external evaluation stage of the business cycle set out in Figure 5 in chapter 4.

Analysing stakeholder expectations will enable common (and contradictory) expectations to be identified. Expectations can be analysed and the level of performance that the organisation is willing to deliver in relation to each of the common expectations can be decided. The core processes established in the organisation will be designed to deliver these expectations to the pre-determined level.

9.1.5   Core Processes

Core processes are groups of related and inter-dependent activities that are the fundament mechanisms for delivering the mission, corporate objectives and stakeholder expectations. Indeed, these core processes arise from and can be fully aligned with the delivery of stakeholder expectations.

Core processes are fundamental to the continued success (or even existence, in its present size and form) of the organisation and the ability to achieve the corporate mission. Each core process creates value in the organisation and is designed to deliver one or more of the stakeholder expectations. The core processes are also fundamentally important to the fulfilment of corporate objectives.

The identification of core processes will need to be undertaken in a co-ordinated manner at corporate level. It would be too fragmented for these processes to be identified by individual departments. There are three basic types of core processes. These are core processes for the:

- continuity and monitoring of routine operations

- management of projects and enhancements

- development and delivery of strategy

A core process delivers one or more stakeholder expectation to the level desired by the organisation. The case studies throughout the book have focussed on the relationship between core processes, key dependencies and the associated risks. Figure B1 in Appendix B provides details of the main core processes that are likely to exist in a premiership football team, such as Whitechapel Football Club (Whitechapel FC).

9.1.6   Key Dependencies

The core processes are supported by the key dependencies and these can be impacted by the significant risks. The impact of the significant risks can be to enhance, inhibit or cause doubt about the key dependency. A key dependency is something that must be present to support a core process. The key dependencies may be internal or external to the organisation.

The FIRM Risk Scorecard is a useful structure for the identification of the key dependencies that support each of the core processes. It is now possible to list the high level dependencies that support the mission, corporate objectives, stakeholder expectations and core processes. These key dependencies can be recorded in a risk matrix. The risk matrix can be structured using the headings of the FIRM Risk Scorecard. Table 7 sets out the partially populated risk matrix for Whitechapel FC. The risk matrix provides a mechanism for reducing the chances of risk overload in the organisation, because it presents a framework within which risks can be placed. It is not unusual for organisations to identify between 100 and 200 risks for inclusion in the risk matrix.

The main reason for identifying key dependencies is to provide an agreed basis on which to raise risk awareness in the organisation. It is worth noting that the lack of common understanding and lack of information for decision making are, themselves, suggested as separate risks by many consultants. Key dependencies support the core processes that deliver the mission, corporate objectives and stakeholder expectations. Risk management must ensure that the risks that could impact these key dependencies have optimal outcomes, when a risk materialises.

Throughout the book, it has been stated that seeking to attach risks to corporate objectives is incorrect, because the objectives are too high level to act as an attachment point. The intermediate steps between corporate objectives and significant risks (in the risk productivity approach) are stakeholder expectations, core processes and key dependencies. However, this full analysis will be too burdensome for many organisations.

The compromise may be to move directly from corporate objectives to key dependencies and then attach risks to the key dependencies. This short cut is not recommended, but at least the risks will be viewed in the correct context as being attached to key dependencies, even if the stakeholder expectations and core processes have not been fully analysed.

Undertaking steps 4, 5 and 6 completes the
"evaluating the risk environment"
or the holistic phase of risk productivity

9.1.7   Significant Risks

A risk is potentially significant if it could impact above the benchmark level for significance and thereby threaten the future existence of the organisation in its present size and form. To be significant to the organisation, the potentially significant risk would have a high or very high likelihood of materialising at (high magnitude) or above (very high magnitude) the benchmark level. Also, a significant risk must have the ability or potential to impact (inhibit, enhance or cause doubt) the key dependencies that support the core processes of the organisation.

In order to confirm that a risk is significant, it needs to be established that it could impact above a pre-determined benchmark of significance. More information on this evaluation procedure is set out in chapter 6. A scoring system can be used to bring better focus to the identification of the priority significant risks, but this is by no means essential.

The identified key dependencies are placed in the risk matrix under the appropriate (or most relevant) heading of the FIRM Risk Scorecard. The risks that could impact the key dependencies can then be identified. Table 7 shows the partially populated risk matrix for Whitechapel FC. Note that the summaries, as written in Table 7, may not be presented as CASE. This is because of the limited space available in the risk matrix boxes.

Key Dependencies	Long term Risks	Medium Term Risks	Short Term Risks
1. Financial	**Procedures Gap:** How successfully do the procedures manage the finances		
1.1 Allocation of funds and capital	Resource allocation Investment policy (F4) Etc	Control of project costs Refurbishment standards Etc	Unpredictable cash flow (F2) Theft and fraud losses Etc
1.2 Procurement arrangements	Procurement strategy (F1) Etc	Purchase agreements (F3) Etc	Supplier failure to deliver Etc
1.3 etc.			
2. Infrastructure	**Process Gap:** How successfully are processes facilitated		
2.1 Administrative and stadium staff Staffing level decision	Training strategy EO Policy standards Etc	Recruitment difficulties (I4) Delivery of training (I2) Etc	Staff behaviour Staff availability (I3) Accidents at work Etc
2.2 The Stadium	Design decisions Etc	Planning permissions Etc	Stadium fire (I1) Bomb scare evacuation Electrical or lighting failure Etc
2.3 etc.			
3. Reputational	**Perception Gap:** How is the organisation perceived by stakeholders		
3.1 Good and consistent match results	Match tactics (R1) Player purchases Etc	Training sessions Etc	Player injuries Etc
3.2 Good Corporate Governance	Marketing strategy (R3) Fair trading policy Visitor numbers Etc	Legal compliance (R4) Etc	Adverse publicity (R2) Unfair trading Etc
3.3 etc.			
4. Marketplace	**Presence Gap:** What is the presence of the organisation in the marketplace		
4.1 Level of merchandise sales	Incorrect merchandise (M1) Business partnerships Etc	Change of supply logistics Inadequate size range Etc	Supply difficulties Pricing decisions (M3) Etc
4.2 Income from proposed Whitechapel TV channel	Marketing strategy Etc	Unsuccessful launch (M2) Advertising campaign (M4) Etc	Broadcasting failure Etc
4.3 etc			

> **Risk Matrix of key dependencies and some of the main risks for WFC**

Table 7: Risk Matrix for Whitechapel FC

The risk matrix lists the risks that could impact the key dependencies that support the core processes. Analysis of the core processes leads to the identification of key dependencies. Many of the core processes will share one or more key dependency. The priority significant risks shown in the risk matrix for Whitechapel FC are discussed and analysed in more detail in the case study in Appendix B. Table B2 in

Appendix B provides more complete definitions of the priority significant risks facing Whitechapel FC.

9.1.8 Risk Priorities

It is not possible to improve the management of all of the risks facing an organisation at the same time. This would require the allocation of considerable resources to the extent that actions may cease to be cost-effective. There needs to be a more structured approach, so that the priority significant risks receive earliest attention.

Section 2 in chapter 6 set out a simple approach to the identification of the priority significant risks facing an organisation, as follows:

1. if the risk has high or very high magnitude in relation to the benchmark test for significance, then it is potentially significant

2. if the risk has a high or very high likelihood of materialising at or above the benchmark level, then it is confirmed as significant

3. if there is high or very high scope for cost effective improvement in control, then the risk is a priority significant risk

A variation on this approach to the production of the list of priority significant risks is to identify the potentially significant risks, as in the first step above and then ask whether the likelihood of the risk materialising at the benchmark level is currently Unknown, High, Medium or Low, taking account of the controls in place. A colour coding can be introduced, as follows:

- Blue   Unknown
- Red   High
- Amber   Medium
- Green   Low

This BRAG coding system can be used in the risk register to provide a visual presentation of the risk profile of the organisation.

For organisations that wish to use a scoring system, the risks in the risk matrix can be assessed, in terms of magnitude (M), likelihood (L) and scope (S) for improved control. Note the following:

Magnitude (M) x Likelihood (L) = Risk Significance
Risk Significance x Scope (S)   = Risk Priority

Table 7 in chapter 6 is a diagrammatic representation of risk priorities. These are the priority significant risks that require further analysis and detailed monitoring.

When the risk priorities have been identified, the organisation can review the results at head office. If one department has a disproportionate number of priority significant risks, then the organisation will need to respond to that situation. It may be that the organisation will decide to out-source the activities of that department. This action will change the risk profile of the organisation and bring the risk profile more into line with the:

- risk attitude of the board;
- risk capacity of the organisation; and
- risk exposure that is acceptable

9.1.9 Analysis of Significant Risks

A detailed analysis of each of the priority significant risks is necessary, so that the risk productivity approach can deliver the available benefits. There is a need to analyse each risk, so that the details can be entered in the risk register. The suggested analysis of priority significant risks is set out in Table 4 in chapter 6. The use of a risk register to record the priority significant risks is discussed later in this chapter.

The production of a risk register that includes an analysis of each of the priority significant risks should ensure that risk management is aligned with all aspects of management activities. Part of the risk analysis is a consideration of the cost of the controls already in place and an evaluation of whether these costs are realistic and appropriate. All of the priority significant risks will have a lifetime and a lifecycle within the organisation. The risk register will track each priority significant risk until it is retired from the risk register, because it is no longer a priority significant risk.

Undertaking steps 7, 8 and 9 completes the
"aligning the significant risks"
or the alignment phase of risk productivity

9.1.10   Risk Capacity

The risk capacity of the organisation is the maximum resource that the organisation is willing to put at risk. It should be agreed by the board and can be treated as the benchmark that is used to evaluate the current risk exposure of the organisation. The component parts of the risk capacity are:

- Hazard Tolerance;

- Control Acceptance; and

- Opportunity Appetite

This approach assumes that risk capacity is a single transferable commodity that can be calculated and quantified. One of the conclusions that may be reached at the end of the risk productivity analysis is that the risk capacity is not correctly allocated between the four headings of the FIRM Risk Scorecard. There may also be an inappropriate allocation of risk capacity between hazard tolerance, control acceptance and opportunity appetite.

The risk exposure for the organisation is the total value that is currently at risk. This should be compared with the risk capacity to decide whether the organisation is taking more (or less) risk than the board is willing to accept. The risk exposure is the total of the individual current risk values (or magnitudes) for all of the significant risks. When calculating risk exposure, the sum of the individual values at risk may overstate the actual risk exposure of the organisation. The sum of the individual values at risk should be adjusted to take account of the degree of correlation between risks. In the case of risks that are not correlated, adding the values at risk may be an over-estimate, because the organisation does not expect (with a 99% level of certainty), that all of the risks will materialise in the same period

The basis of the analysis is that hazard tolerance, control acceptance and opportunity appetite can be added together to form the risk capacity of the organisation. Risk capacity is considered to be a single transferable commodity that can be allocated to the headings and re-allocated in light of detailed analysis. It can also be consciously and deliberately allocated between hazard tolerance, control acceptance and opportunity appetite. So, if an organisation wishes to use a large proportion of its risk capacity in pursuit of marketplace opportunities, then it will have less risk capacity available for hazard risks. Control risks will always be a less volatile area of risk and it is usually a more fixed component of the total risk exposure (and risk capacity) of the organisation.

Risk capacity is not usually defined and quantified by the organisation. The risk capacity is the cumulative willingness to accommodate risk within the organisation. There is a need for the board to discuss and agree the risk capacity of the organisation, so that all of the available risk capacity is used to full advantage. Also, the organisation needs to be satisfied that the current level of risk exposure (adjusted for risk correlation) does not exceed the risk capacity of the organisation.

This approach to risk capacity will also help develop a dynamic approach to risk and risk management. The organisation should view its corporate resources as made up of three component parts:

- Reserves;

- Revenue; and

- Risk

Each key dependency in the organisation will also have these components of reserve, revenue and risk. Chapter 1 explored this concept in more detail and suggested that it is only the "Risk", or "at risk" component of the key dependency that will substantially benefit form the application of risk management tools and techniques. It is likely that early attempts by the organisation to quantify risks in this way will be difficult, although value at risk analyses are becoming more common and the available tools and techniques are becoming more robust.

9.1.11 Response to Significant Risks

Risk response is a well established stage in the discipline of risk management. Following the identification of the significant risks during the risk assessment exercise, it is necessary to respond to the priority significant risks. Responses to the priority significant risks include:

- accept or retain

- avoid or eliminate

- neutralise or hedge

- control or reduce

- insure or transfer

The structured nature of the risk productivity approach means that a more analytical basis for the selection of appropriate risk responses can now be achieved. Organisations should look at the full range of risks that it faces and determine the risk responses in a more co-ordinated and consistent manner.

It is the case that most risks will have an impact under more than one heading of the FIRM Risk Scorecard. Each risk will have been placed under the heading where the impact would be greatest. Therefore, the following analysis should be treated as being empirical, or a first approximation. The stages in this more integrative and sophisticated approach are as follows:

1. Define risk capacity as the maximum value at risk that the organisation is willing to accept and undertake an exercise to quantify the risk capacity of the organisation

2. Illustrate this risk capacity by using the FIRM Risk Scorecard as in Figure 6 in chapter 5 and confirm that the presentation represents the attitude of the board

3. Analyse the individual priority significant risks to determine the current risk exposure and the actual allocation of risk capacity (value at risk) to each of these priority significant risks

4. Check that adding the individual values at risk together does not over-stated the risk exposure, because many of the risks are not correlated, then adjust the risk exposure figure(s)

5. Include the values at risk for individual priority significant risks on the FIRM Risk Scorecard to show the actual allocation of risk capacity to the priority significant risks at current risk levels

6. Determine what re-distribution of risk capacity within the FIRM Risk Scorecard is required to ensure full and appropriate use and allocation of the risk capacity

This approach will enable the organisation to determine how much capacity is available under each of the headings of the FIRM Risk Scorecard and how much is currently utilised under each heading. The organisation will also be able to calculate the actual risk exposure and determine whether the values currently at risk are consistent with the declared risk capacity of the organisation. This approach will ensure that the risk capacity is fully and properly allocated. The outcomes from this analysis will lead to decisions about the risk productivity indicators (RPIs) to be used, so that the utilisation of risk capacity is carefully and accurately monitored. Also, the benefits of fully utilising the risk capacity can then be quantified.

9.1.12   Risk Productivity Indicators

Most organisations use key performance indicators (KPIs) as a means of tracking performance against targets. When the measurement is risk based, then it is important for management to recognise that fact. Recognition of the risk-based nature of the relevant measurements will help focus attention on the importance of risk. The way to bring this about is to designate these risk based KPIs as risk productivity indicators (or RPIs).

The basis of the approach is to achieve maximum risk productivity in the organisation. If a heading of the FIRM Risk Scorecard is utilising insufficient risk capacity, then more risk can be transferred to that heading, or the decision can be consciously taken to transfer that spare risk capacity to another risk heading. In order to be satisfied that the organisation is gaining full benefit from its risk capacity, there are a number of questions that could be asked, including:

1.   does the organisation take as much risk as it should

2.   are RPIs allocated to appropriate priority significant risks

3.   has risk been considered as a positive (appetite) issue

4.   are risks managed in the context that gave rise to the risks

5.   is the risk register used as a reference document by management

6.   is the link to core processes and key dependencies understood

7.   are all useful risk management tools and techniques used

8.   are criteria of success employed for opportunity risks

When the twelve steps to risk productivity have been completed, then risk management will be fully embedded into the management of the organisation. The understanding of risk capacity in the organisation should help with strategic decisions. The allocation of the risk capacity should be deliberate and dynamic, rather than based on historical attitudes to risk.

Regular review of the risk profile and the periodic monitoring of risks will remain the responsibility of the audit committee. The audit committee will focus its attention on the review of those KPIs that have been identified as risk based, by the allocation of risk productivity indicators (RPIs) to the measurement of risk performance. The audit committee will also need to set the parameters for reporting cases of non-compliance with the risk management protocols. It is the risk management committee that will take the lead in deciding the pro-active allocation of risk capacity, in consultation with the board.

Undertaking steps 10, 11 and 12 completes the
"embedding appropriate actions"
or the embedding phase of risk productivity

9.2. Risk Register

Details of the priority significant risks will need to be recorded in a consistent format that adds to the successful management of these risks. The risk register has already been mentioned as the document where details of the priority significant risks are recorded. The corporate risk register should be managed in a way that does not give the impression to local management that the responsibility for managing the priority significant risks has, in any way, been transferred to corporate head office.

Each risk needs to be analysed in detail, so that information can be entered in the risk register. This will ensure that risk management is embedded into all aspects of the management of the core processes. The risk register will contain details of the priority significant risks faced by the organisation. The information contained in the risk register defines the risk profile of the organisation. The risk register will contain details of the analysis of each of the significant risks, including the risk productivity indicators (RPIs) allocated to each of these priority significant risks.

Table B2 in Appendix B is an illustration of the contents or summary page of a risk register. The main part of the register will be the individual pages that set out the detailed analysis of each of the priority significant risks in turn.

The risk productivity approach can be applied to project management. The application of the approach to project risk management is only discussed in outline in chapter 4. In relation to the risks associated with projects, the priority significant risks will be retired as stages of the project are completed. The archive of project risk registers will serve as record of the risk cycle of each priority significant risk and it will also be a record of the application of risk management tools and techniques to each of the risks. This archive of updated risk registers should form part of the project file.

9.3.   Risk Assurance Management System

A standardised structure for management systems is not yet available, although work is continuing at the International Organisation for Standardization (ISO). The twelve steps to risk productivity discussed in this chapter are not set out as a standard. Nevertheless, the twelve steps, together with the comments on the risk architecture, strategy and protocols and the risk guidelines provide all of the essential sections and elements of a management system.

Typically, a management system will have six sections. In relation to a risk management standard, these could be set out as follows:

- Risk Management Policy
- Preparation and Planning
- Implementation and Operation
- Monitoring of Risk Performance
- Improvement in Risk Management
- Management Review

Each of the sections will have a number of elements. These elements can be reconciled with the elements set out in a typical standard, such as the ISO 9000 series on quality assurance management systems. In general, management systems are written in relation for what could be considered to be equivalent to hazard risks. Therefore, some re-interpretation of the common elements is required. In order to constitute a management system, the contents of a risk assurance management system (RAMS) would be as follows:

1. Risk Management Policy

2. Risk Recognition (Risk Matrix)

3. Identification of Priority Significant Risks

4. Setting of Risk Performance Targets

5. Identification of Risk Resources

6. Risk Architecture

7. Risk Protocols

8. Event Management Plans

9. Risk Control Standards

10. Management of Human Resources

11. Management of Other Resources

12. Documentation and its Control

13. Risk Communications and Training

14. Suppliers and Contractors

15. Monitoring of Risk Performance

16. Management of Non-Conformities

17. Audit Arrangements for Risk Performance

18. Preventive Actions

19. Corrective Actions

20. Continual Improvement in Performance

21. Management Review of RAMS

The risk productivity approach described in this book has all of the essential elements required for a full risk assurance management system or RAMS, even if the structure of the twelve steps to risk productivity is not in accordance with the 21 elements above. The following paragraphs highlight some specific issues.

At the top of the risk management hierarchy is the risk assurance management system (RAMS). It defines the overall approach to the management of risks in the organisation. The twelve steps to achieving risk productivity, together with the risk architecture, strategy and protocols (RASP) define the essential aspects of the RAMS.

Most risk assurance management systems currently in use recommend that the organisation attaches risks directly to corporate objectives. Attempting to attach risks to corporate objectives is incorrect, because the objectives will normally be high level statements that are difficult to evaluate in detail. It is much better to link the risks to the practical and easily understood key dependencies that support the core processes in the organisation. These key dependencies also, of course, support the corporate objectives. The major benefit of linking risks to key dependencies is that there is ownership of dependencies and this ownership can be extended directly to ownership of the risks that could impact a dependency.

When the risk register of priority significant risks has been compiled, the risk manager can validate the risk architecture, strategy and protocols (RASP) for the continuing management of those risks. The RASP can only be established and validated after the risk productivity exercise has been completed, so that the RASP is fully compatible with the priority significant risks. The RASP sets out the administrative aspects of the RAMS.

The risk manager will fulfil the role of guardian of the risk architecture, strategy and protocols (GRASP) and will be concerned with all aspects of risk management and its interface with other aspects of corporate governance, including the work of the audit committee and compliance with Turnbull. At all times, the risk manager will need to liaise with the risk owners and the owners of the core processes. However, it is vitally important that the risk manager distinguishes between risks and management issues, so that risk management does not appear to be trying to take over the whole organisation.

Successful management of risks needs a strong framework or management system. However, a fully developed and implemented framework for the integrative, holistic, aligned and embedded management of all types of risks has not yet been devised and successfully implemented. The twelve steps to risk productivity approach described in this chapter represent the most comprehensive model of a robust RAMS that is currently on offer. It is an approach that can be readily presented in the structure of a RAMS, by aligning the steps to achieving risk productivity with the 21 elements listed previously.

The risk productivity approach has been presented and discussed as an approach that applies to the snapshot of the risk profile of the organisation or department at any one time. The risk productivity approach can also be applied more specifically, as required, to any particular core process, including operations, project and strategy core processes.

Summary and Review of Chapter 9

Chapter 9 sets out the twelve steps involved in achieving risk productivity. The twelve steps to risk productivity, together with the risk architecture, strategy and protocols (RASP) for the organisation, define a fully developed risk assurance management system (RAMS). The overall aim of the approach is to ensure that the organisation is making full use of its risk capacity in a positive way that will enhance the achievement of the mission of the organisation.

Assigning risk productivity indicators (RPIs) to the monitoring of the effectiveness of the key controls will enhance the contribution made by risk management. Assigning RPIs is the final step in the evaluation of the priority significant risks facing the organisation. The RASP should ensure that the twelve steps are successfully and consistently implemented, within the whole organisation and also to individual core processes, of all types.

Risk management is a high profile management initiative at the moment and it is receiving much attention. Even so, efforts to improve the management of risks will be competing with other demands on management time and corporate resources. Accordingly, risk management has to demonstrate that it is a priority area for further action that is capable of delivering worthwhile and lasting benefits.

A structured approach that is aligned and embedded with routine management activities is most likely to be successful. It is suggested that the use of RPIs will assist management, as well as the audit committee, in focussing on the priority significant risks and the monitoring of the key controls.

The main message from this chapter is that risk productivity indicators (RPIs) provide the mechanism for aligning risk management activities with the corporate mission. The style of approach to be used for any specific risk should combine the best from the hazard management, control management and opportunity management styles. Case Study 9 consolidates the key messages outlined in this chapter. The consolidated case study set out in Appendix B illustrates the ideas further.

Case Study 9: Premiership Football Club – (Part 2)

Whitechapel Lakes plc, is the owner of Whitechapel Football Club (Whitechapel FC). It provides an example of how businesses can diversify and thereby achieve further business success. Merchandising and franchising opportunities for Whitechapel FC have been recognised by Whitechapel Lakes plc. Successfully managing this merchandising and franchising operation requires sophisticated risk management focus and effort.

The "good selection of merchandise for football supporters" core process is being designed. This core process will have a number of dependencies that can be impacted by the following types of risks:

* hazard risks that could inhibit the achievement of success in the merchandising and franchising business;

* control risks that could introduce doubt about the ability to successfully deliver the process; and

* opportunity risks that could enhance the delivery of the process and make it more successful

In order to track risk management performance, risk productivity indicators (RPIs) need to be agreed. The range of RPIs that will be introduced should track the values at risk within this core process. The RPIs should be designed to provide reassurance that the process is working well, and/or provide early warning that risks are moving outside the acceptable range of performance.

The "good selection of merchandise for football supporters" core process will have substantial reputational aspects. Whitechapel FC will need to be satisfied that the reputational value at risk has been fully understood. Overall, Whitechapel Lakes plc has to be satisfied that Whitechapel FC has sufficient risk capacity to be able to undertake the development work that is required to successfully fulfil this core process. Alternatively, Whitechapel Lakes plc could utilise some group risk capacity to assist Whitechapel FC.

10

Review of Key Messages

Risk Capacity should be fully utilised and correctly allocated by the organisation, to support achievement of the corporate mission

This chapter summarises and consolidates the ideas and concepts set out in earlier chapters. The key messages are that risk management must be aligned with the corporate mission and that management of risks should be embedded into routine management activities. It is not possible to move directly from a statement of corporate objectives to the identification of the priority significant risks. Attempting to do this will result in the identification of risks in isolation from the core processes of the organisation.

The importance of risk capacity is emphasised. This has been mentioned throughout the book. The risk capacity of an organisation is the sum of the hazard tolerance plus control acceptance plus opportunity appetite. The importance of this concept is that an organisation can determine whether its actual risk exposure is greater than is acceptable to the board. Also, the organisation can decide if it is using too much of its risk capacity on hazard risks or if it is using too much risk capacity under one particular heading of the FIRM Risk Scorecard.

The organisation should make full use of its risk capacity if it is to achieve the corporate mission. Apart from the dangers of incorrectly allocating risk capacity, there is also the danger of not making full use of the available risk capacity in the organisation. The risk productivity approach will help organisations avoid under-utilisation of the full risk capacity available within the organisation. The approach will also assist with the monitoring of corporate risk performance, by the allocation of risk productivity indicators (RPIs) to risk based performance measurements.

10.1. Chapter Messages

Each chapter addresses an important aspect of the discipline of risk management and puts forward a key message to summarise the ideas and concepts discussed in the chapter. Table 8 sets out the key messages for easy reference.

The extended case study in Appendix B builds on the ideas put forward throughout the book and, in particular, the twelve steps to achieving risk productivity outlined in chapter 9. Appendix B also draws these key messages together into a coherent and co-ordinated

Chapter	Key Message
1.	Do not manage risks out of context, or in isolation from the situation that gave rise to the risks
2	Risk Management improves the management of the core processes of the organisation by optimising risk outcomes
3.	Risk Management will bring benefits at whichever level of sophistication the organisation implements the discipline
4.	Risk Management must be aligned with the mission of the organisation in order to achieve lasting benefits
5.	The FIRM Risk Scorecard ensures robust risk assessment and facilitates the allocation of risk capacity
6.	A risk is significant if it could impact above the benchmark level for significance and thereby threaten the existence of the organisation
7.	Risk Guidelines that include a framework of responsibilities will facilitate management of significant risks within the organisation
8.	Risk Manager must develop the role in order to become the Guardian of the Risk Architecture, Strategy and Protocols (GRASP)
9.	Risk Productivity Indicators (RPIs) provide the mechanism for aligning risk management activities with the corporate mission
10.	Risk Capacity should be fully utilised and correctly allocated by the organisation, to support achievement of the corporate mission

> **The chapter messages help to explain the
> Risk Productivity approach**

Table 8: Chapter Messages

framework. The messages help to build an approach that forms the framework of a risk assurance management system (RAMS), based on an overall approach referred to as "Risk Productivity".

10.1.1 Management of Risks in Context

Chapter 1 discussed the nature of risk and presented the key message that risks should not be managed out of context, or in isolation from the situation that gave rise to the risks.

Section 1 set out some of the basic issues for consideration in relation to the definition of risk. Risks can affect achievement of the mission by impacting the key dependencies that support the core processes. The core processes deliver the stakeholder expectations and the corporate objectives, as well as the corporate mission.

Section 2 examined the historical differentiation between the management of hazard risks, control risks and opportunity risks. The suggestion is that all risks can be managed in a similar manner, whether they are of a hazard, control or opportunity nature.

10.1.2 Management of Core Processes

Chapter 2 discussed the nature of risk management and presented the key message that risk management improves the management of core processes within the organisation.

Section 1 set out some of the basic issues for consideration in relation to the nature of the risk management discipline. There are seven clearly defined and inter-dependent stages involved in the risk management discipline. These seven stages build to create five risk management activities that have a range of useful outputs. Risk management should not be viewed as a stand alone discipline. It must be aligned with other management activities and responsibilities.

Section 2 examined the risk management stages in terms of the activities, the outputs and the professionals who will have a contribution to make. All contributions should be focused on assisting risk owners in the fulfilment of their obligations to the organisation in relation to the risks for which they have stewardship.

10.1.3 Level of Sophistication

Chapter 3 discussed the various styles of risk management and presented the key message that risk management need only be as sophisticated as the organisation requires in order to bring benefits.

Section 1 set out the three different styles of risk management. All three styles will need to be applied in an organisation. It is also worth noting that the different types of risks have historically been managed in different ways and this differentiation continues to be valid. In fact, the same risk will often have all three styles applied to it by the organisation during the life cycle of the risk.

Section 2 examined the different levels of sophistication that can be applied and all levels will produce a positive contribution at any one time. Where the nature of the risk allows, the intention is to move the response to the risk from Reform to Conform to Perform, as illustrated in Figure 4.

10.1.4 Alignment of Risk Management

Chapter 4 discussed embedding risk management and presented the key message that risk management must be aligned with the mission of the organisation in order to achieve lasting benefits.

Section 1 identified the expectations of stakeholders and the processes that deliver those expectations. Risk management tools and techniques can then be firmly embedded into the continuation of normal operation, the execution of projects and the formulation of strategy. However, corporate objectives do not represent the best basis for identification of significant risks. These objectives will often be stated as annual, internal, change objectives.

Section 2 examined the need to embed risk management into operations, projects and strategy. The best chance of embedding risk management into corporate processes is to fully align the risk management activities with the timetable for departmental reporting and other corporate diary events and activities.

10.1.5 FIRM Risk Scorecard

Chapter 5 discussed the classification of risks and presented the key message that the Financial – Infrastructure – Reputational – Marketplace (FIRM) Risk Scorecard ensures robust risk assessment.

Section 1 set out some of the basic issues for consideration in relation to the timescales for the impact of risks. Short term, medium term and long term risks are identified. Different organisations will allocate different timescales to short term, medium term and long term impact, depending on the size and nature of the organisation.

Section 2 introduced the FIRM Risk Scorecard as a valuable tool for demonstrating the inter-dependent nature of risk and the integrative nature of risk management. The FIRM Risk Scorecard was presented as having four headings:

- Financial
- Infrastructure
- Reputational
- Marketplace

Consideration of the attributes of the FIRM Risk Scorecard enables easier understanding of many of the ideas and concept supporting risk productivity. These attributes are listed in Table 3.

10.1.6 Significant Risks

Chapter 6 discussed the identification of priority significant risks and presented the key message that a risk is significant if it could impact above the benchmark level for significance and thereby threaten the future existence of the organisation in its present size and form. A significant risk will be capable of impacting one or more of the following, either directly or indirectly:

- key dependencies
- continuity of core processes
- delivery of stakeholder expectations
- fulfilment of corporate objectives
- achievement of the corporate mission

Section 1 discussed mechanisms for the identification of priority significant risks. The approach is based on the development of the FIRM Risk Scorecard as a means of risk recognition. A key area of concern for many organisations is that they will fail to recognise all of the risks that could impact the key dependencies in the organisation.

The FIRM Risk Scorecard is a means of ensuring that all potentially significant risks are identified.

Section 2 discussed the fact that the identification of significant risks cannot be undertaken in isolation from the processes that could be impacted by the risks. It is important to establish the benchmark test for significance under each of the four headings of the FIRM Risk Scorecard. The analysis will also facilitate the identification of the core processes that are significantly at risk, and/or at greatest risk.

10.1.7 Risk Guidelines

Chapter 7 discussed risk management responsibilities and the need for risk guidelines. It also presented the key message that a robust framework of responsibilities is required for the management of the priority significant risks within the organisation. The framework is related to the risk architecture, strategy and protocols (RASP). The RASP represents the administrative aspects of the overall risk assurance management system (RAMS).

Section 1 explored many of the issues associated with establishing a suitable risk management structure or architecture. The fundamental objective to be achieved is that the risk management structure is aligned with business imperatives, business strategy and budget formulation. The structure should also be aligned (and embedded) with the management of the core processes.

Section 2 suggested contents for the Risk Guidelines. These will provide information on how people within the organisation should fulfil their risk management responsibilities. The guidelines and the risk management policy can be structured to reflect the five activities that make up the risk management discipline.

10.1.8 RASP and the Risk Manager

Chapter 8 discussed the relationship between risk and the risk manager and presented the key message that the role of the risk manager must develop to become the guardian of the risk architecture, strategy and protocols (GRASP).

Section 1 discussed the changed and expanded role of the risk manager. It is no longer viable to expect the risk manager to be an expert in all the risks that may be faced by the organisation. Despite years of experience that can be brought to bear on a specific class of risk, the risk agenda is now too wide to be within the expertise of one individual. The contribution that the risk manager can make is that of guardian of the risk architecture, strategy and protocols. The sponsor of the risk assurance management system should be a board director and it is likely that the GRASP will report to that board director.

Section 2 examined the role of the risk manager as guardian of the risk architecture, strategy and protocols (GRASP). The strategy is the description of what needs to be achieved with respect to risk. The protocols are the systems and procedures by which the strategy is fulfilled and the architecture is the risk structure, including the means of communication, that has been put in place in the organisation.

10.1.9 Risk Productivity Indicators

Chapter 9 discussed the steps involved in achieving risk productivity and presented the key message that risk productivity indicators (RPIs) provide the mechanism for aligning risk management activities with the corporate mission.

Chapter 9 set out the twelve steps involved in achieving risk productivity. The overall aim of the approach is to ensure that the organisation is making full use of its risk capacity in a positive way that will enhance the achievement of the mission of the organisation.

Although the risk productivity approach may be most beneficial when applied to opportunity risks, some risk capacity will always need to be allocated to hazard tolerance. This is because an organisation has to accept that hazard risks are an inescapable part of its activities. Assigning risk productivity indicators (RPIs) as a means of monitoring the effectiveness of the controls applied to priority significant risks that support the key dependencies will enhance the contribution made by risk management.

10.1.10 Risk Capacity

Chapter 10 provides a review of the key messages and consolidates the ideas presented. It also presents the key message that the organisation should make full use of its risk capacity to achieve the corporate mission. Appendix B provides an illustrated consolidation of the ideas put forward throughout the book.

Section 1 reviewed the key messages set out in each of the earlier chapters. The overall message is that risk capacity should be correctly allocated by the organisation, if the corporate mission is to be achieved. Full use of risk capacity is a fundamental aspect of the risk productivity approach.

Section 2 examined the current status of the discipline of risk management. In order to assist with the understanding and successful implementation of the risk productivity approach, specific meanings are assigned to the following phases of risk management:

- integrative;

- holistic;

- aligned; and

- embedded

Understanding the different aspects of the discipline of risk management enables organisations to gain the maximum benefits.

10.2. Risk Management and the Mission

Risk management is an important management initiative at the moment. It is currently a high profile initiative, because there is no doubt that risks have increased in the business environment. There are many recent and continuing developments that make the business environment a much riskier place:

- greater transparency required from organisations

- pace of change in business ever increasing

- regulatory pressures continue to increase

- changing commercial and marketplace environment

- globalisation of markets and products

- increased competition in the marketplace

- joint ventures becoming more common and more complex

- high profile losses and failures ruin reputations

- convergence of markets and expectations

- need to respond more rapidly to stakeholder expectations

- more volatile markets with less customer loyalty

- impact of e-commerce on all aspects of business life

- reputation becomes more and more important

- diversification leads to working in unfamiliar areas

- desire to deliver greater shareholder value

- constant need to make bold strategic decisions

- short term success required, without long term detriment

- product innovation and continuous improvement required

Risk management adds shareholder value by creating a greater likelihood of fulfilling the stakeholder expectations, business objectives and corporate mission. Risk management can also assist with the achievement of competitive advantage. It will add value by providing a reduction in the management time spent on crisis management. It should also provide a lower cost of capital and a higher share price over the time. In short, enhanced risk management will greatly assist achievement of the mission.

Many words are used to describe the new and developing approach to risk management. If risk management is to be fully and successfully implemented, then these words need to be evaluated and the concepts behind the words should be implemented to the extent that is beneficial for the organisation. In short, risk management needs to be:

- integrative;

- holistic;

- aligned; and

- embedded

The overall intention is to make risk management more dynamic and proactive. In brief outline, the four phases of risk management listed above can be described in the following ways:

- **Integrative Risk Management** means that risks are managed in a way that integrates the activities of all parties who have responsibilities for the management of risks within the organisation. Integrative risk management will enable the organisation to prepare itself in anticipation of the introduction of risk productivity.

- **Holistic Risk Management** means that the management of risks encompasses all possible risks, including the types of risks described under the four headings of the FIRM Risk Scorecard. Holistic risk management will enable the organisation to evaluate the risk environment within which it operates.

- **Aligned Risk Management** means risk management activities are aligned with the timetable for the various aspects of the business cycle in the organisation and the activities support achievement of the business plan, strategy plan and annual budget. Aligned risk management will ensure that risk management activities operate in support of other business activities within the organisation.

- **Embedded Risk Management** means that management of risks is embedded into the business cycle in the organisation and risk management is embedded into preparation of project plans and operating procedures. Embedded risk management will result in the actions taken in support of risk management becoming accepted as a necessary and beneficial part of normal business activities.

Risk reporting under Turnbull can also be facilitated within the risk productivity framework. Routine feedback will be required from the risk owners and from the core process owners. This feedback will form the basis of reports to the audit committee and also the basis of the Turnbull compliance procedures. These Turnbull procedures will also help define the role and priorities of the internal audit function.

When a fully integrative, holistic, aligned and embedded approach has been achieved in an organisation, the following features will be present:

- risk will be managed in context

- risk capacity will be fully utilised

- risk register will be a dynamic document

- risk management will be making a valuable contribution

- risk management will be making a valued contribution

- management of key dependencies will be pro-active

- entrepreneurial appetite will not be suppressed

- control risks will not be over-managed

10.2.1 Integrative Risk Management

Integrative risk management is the first phase in the introduction of risk productivity. It is shown in Figure 9 as having the following stages:

- agree mission of organisation
- establish corporate objectives
- identify important stakeholders

"Integrated Risk Management" is a commonly used phrase to describe this part of the risk productivity approach. However, a better description is "Integrative Risk Management", because integrative indicates that a forward looking attitude is required. The RASP that is implemented in the organisation should be creative and exhaustive, not something that is created and exhausted. Risk management must be integrative (active and dynamic) and not integrated (reactive and static).

Turnbull requires organisations to take actions that can only be fully achieved if there is an embedded approach combined with a forward looking integrative mentality. Many organisations are rethinking their risk management structures and approaches. The implementation of enhanced risk management protocols will be most successful if they are integrative.

One of the key factors in the effective introduction of risk management and internal control is the creation of a risk management culture in the minds of all staff. This will change risk management from an implicit responsibility of the few to an explicit responsibility of all. Internal control is a key element in managing risk and internal control systems must also follow a risk based approach.

10.2.2 Holistic Risk Management

Holistic risk management is the second phase in the introduction of risk productivity. It is shown in Figure 9 as having the following stages:

- establish stakeholder expectations
- confirm and/or create core processes
- identify key dependencies

The risk management approach must encompass a consideration of all risks. An approach based on the FIRM Risk Scorecard will facilitate such a holistic approach. The approach must be holistic in that all risks are considered and holistic in that all appropriate risk management tools and techniques are fully utilised.

An organisation needs to achieve its mission and corporate objectives. There is also a need to manage the organisation so that the best interests of stakeholders are protected. Therefore, risk management is an integral part of corporate governance. When the approach to risk management is fully holistic, a common language will also exist. Note that the language of risk used throughout this book is set out in Appendix A "Definitions and Terminology".

If the risk management initiative is to be successful, then it needs to be compatible with current business thinking. The business case for risk management must be based on such concepts as value propositions, compliance, project management, soft issues, control of the business processes, ownership and accountability, business risk profile, balance of risk and reward, support of strategic aims, provision of specialist skills and a recognition of potential cost savings.

10.2.3 Aligned Risk Management

Aligned risk management is the third phase in the introduction of risk productivity. It is shown in Figure 9 as having the following stages:

- determine significant risks
- identify risk priorities
- analyse priority significant risks

Risk management activities must be aligned with achievement of the mission if the full benefits are to be achieved. Aligning risk management with the business cycle in the organisation will require that the cycle of risk management activities provides structured risk management input into formulation of (at least) the following:

- strategy plans
- annual budget
- performance reviews
- Audit Committee meetings

Risk management can add most value if the cycle of risk management activities is aligned with the corporate calendar. Provided that risk management aligns its activities with the submission dates for departmental reports, then full attention will be paid to risks in strategy formulation and budget planning activities.

When risk monitoring is fully aligned with process monitoring activities, there is no longer any need for the risk monitoring stage to be seen as a separate and/or distinct risk management activity. The use of risk productivity indicators (RPIs) will assist with the alignment of risk management and the monitoring of risk performance. Additionally, it will always be necessary for a review of risk management activities, the risk register, the RASP and the RAMS to be undertaken and/or coordinated in a formal manner. The audit committee will undertake this work, if the organisation has such a group.

10.2.4 Embedded Risk Management

Embedded risk management is the final phase in the introduction of risk productivity. It is shown in Figure 9 as having the following stages:

- confirm allocation of risk capacity

- agree response to significant risks

- establish risk productivity indicators

Risk management activities must be embedded into corporate activities or the full benefits will not be achieved. Many organisations are seeking to implement "objectives-driven" risk management. That means that the organisation uses the corporate objectives as the starting point for risk assessment and (perhaps) the end point for risk review. This approach is likely to fail, because it is difficult to move from objectives to the identification of the priority significant risks in one step. This involves moving directly form the "establish corporate objectives" step (item 2) in Figure 9 to the "determine significant risks" step (item 7). This approach omits the holistic (evaluating the risk environment) phase of risk productivity altogether.

The risk productivity approach is based on an analysis of the core processes that are supported by key dependencies that can be impacted by risks. The approach can be described as "dependencies-driven". This approach is more likely to be successful, because it can be more easily embedded into corporate activities. It is unhelpful to separate risk management from effective management of the organisation.

"Objectives-driven" risk management is more likely to remove risks from the context that gave rise to the risks, because the objectives may not be owned by all staff in a department. Core processes and key dependencies are more likely to be owned by individual departments.

Risk management responsibilities should be embedded into job descriptions. When fully embedded into the activities of the organisation, risk management will ensure acceptance of the risk productivity indicators (RPIs), facilitate ownership of risks and enable the risk manager to operate as guardian of the risk architecture, strategy and protocols (GRASP).

Embedded risk management will be successful when priority significant risks are explicitly analysed, rather than being implicitly taken for granted. Remember that the positive act of accepting a risk is not the same as the negative act of ignoring it. If risk management is providing a framework for the explicit consideration of risks and if this framework is dynamic, then it will become truly embedded into the management of the organisation.

10.3. Future for Risk Management

Risks can be good, uncertain or bad, but they are always inevitable. Risk is a continuum and risks can change from hazard to control to opportunity at different times in the same organisation. It is, therefore, sensible to consider risk as a single commodity that need not be separated into different components for management purposes. Likewise, risk capacity is a single transferable commodity. Risk, together with the reserves and revenue make up the total resources of the organisation, as discussed in chapter 1.

The historic approach of viewing hazard risks separate from control and opportunity risks is increasingly restrictive, if the organisation wishes to gain maximum benefit from its risk portfolio. The risk productivity approach to risk capacity also demonstrates the concepts of inter-dependency and aggregation of risks.

The discipline of risk management continues to be a high profile management initiative. There are four options for any organisation with respect to the new risk management agenda:

- refuse to adopt any of the aspects of the discipline
- do the minimum Turnbull compliance (if mandatory)

- try the approach, but abandon it, if no immediate benefits arise

- continue with the initiative until benefits are delivered

Risk management must become integrative, holistic, aligned and embedded, if it is to make a worthwhile contribution. When the organisation decides to embrace risk productivity, there will be a need to achieve the full benefits from all four phases. Progress with the implementation of the initiative is likely to occur to the following timescale within an organisation:

• organising for risk management and and setting up the appropriate risk architecture, strategy and protocols	**Integrative phase** **3 to 6 months**
• evaluating the risk environment to establish the stakeholder expectations, core processes and key dependencies	**Holistic phase** **6 to 12 months**
• alignment of risk management to identify and analyse the priority significant risks facing the organisation	**Alignment phase** **1 to 2 years**
• embedding risk management into all activities of the organisation by introducing risk productivity indicators	**Embedding phase** **2 to 5 years**

Risk management will be driven by a number of issues in the future. There will always be a need for adequate hazard management and the traditional insurance based risk management skills will continue to be vitally important. Also, control management will continue to be a necessary feature of the way that control risks are managed. However, mechanisms will need to be put in place to ensure that the control management mentality does not suppress the entrepreneurial mentality of the organisation.

Now that the discipline of risk management has become fashionable, it has also become desirable. Because it is desirable, many professionals and disciplines now claim ownership of the risk management agenda. There is a danger that the group of professionals that becomes dominant in the practice of risk management over the next few years, will adopt an approach that is to the exclusion of other disciplines who have an important contribution to make.

As risk management moves from its historical close links with insurance to a clear alignment with core business processes, the contribution that risk management can make will increase. However, if risk management is seen as a separate discipline, then the responsibility for the management of the priority significant risks and the ownership of those risks will become unclear.

By undertaking the risk productivity approach described in this book, an organisation will be able to achieve the following:

- risk management aligned with mission
- risks management becomes more relevant
- risks managed effectively and in context
- better maintenance of core processes
- better delivery of stakeholder expectations
- clear identification of the key dependencies
- delivery of the corporate objectives
- focus for internal audit priorities and activities
- development from Reform to Conform to Perform
- RPIs embedded into monitoring of core processes
- risk management as an aid to decision making
- risk capacity quantified and understood
- RAMS designed and implemented
- allocation of risk capacity in line with board attitude
- "Risk Productivity" achieved

Summary and Review of Chapter 10

Section 1 reviews the key messages set out in each of the earlier chapters. The overall message is that an embedded approach to the management of risks will ensure achievement of the benefits of risk productivity.

The organisation needs to make an evaluation of what the discipline of risk management can provide by way of substantial benefits. It is very important that the scale of the task is fully evaluated and the different approaches that are available are carefully explored, before management time and effort is expended.

Section 2 examines the current status of the discipline of risk management and ascribed different meanings to each of the terms integrative, holistic, aligned and embedded risk management. It is suggested that greater understanding of the different aspects of the discipline of risk management will enable an organisation to gain the maximum benefits.

The overall importance of the risk productivity approach is that it will enable organisations to focus on the following:

- robust identification of priority significant risks

- utilisation of the full risk capacity of the organisation

- development of risks from hazard to control to opportunity

- transfer of risk capacity within the FIRM Risk Scorecard

- RPIs embedded into the monitoring of core processes

- risk management as an aid to decision making

The main message from this chapter is that the organisation should make full use of its risk capacity to achieve the corporate mission. The styles of risk management that develop within the organisation should be based on adopting and then adapting those aspects of the overall risk productivity approach that will benefit the organisation. Case Study 10 consolidates the key messages outlined in this chapter.

Case Study 10: Personal Risk Profile – (Part 2)

The case study in chapter 5 considered the need for Russell Square to use part of his risk capacity to buy a replacement car. This case study takes a broader view of the personal circumstances of Mr Square. It considers the start of the process that will enable him to quantify his personal risk capacity and then make his lifestyle choices.

He has identified that the stakeholders in his life are:

- Partner
- Friends
- Employer
- Colleagues
- Service Providers
- Government

Russell has listed the stakeholder expectations and the personal core processes to deliver those expectations. The analysis that he undertook next was the identification of the key dependencies that support his core processes. He decided that the fundamental question to be answered under each heading of the FIRM Risk Scorecard, together with the two most important key dependencies are as follows:

Financial   "How well do my procedures manage my finances"
- performance of my investments
- level of my ongoing expenditure

Infrastructure   "How well does my body facilitate my processes"
- current state of my health
- my emotional well-being

Reputational   "How am I perceived by my peer group"
- personal characteristics and behaviour
- professional status and reputation

Marketplace   "What is my presence in the marketplace"
- occupation or profession
- current level of income

Russell can now populate his personal risk matrix and move to the identification of his priority significant risks, followed by decisions on risk capacity and its allocation. Finally, he will be able to select RPIs to monitor his lifestyle. These RPIs can then be aligned with his behaviour and embedded into his lifestyle.

Appendices

Appendix A

Definitions and Terminology

Every organisation needs to establish a common understanding and language of risk

1. **Benchmark**
   A risk will be potentially significant if it has the ability to impact
   above an identified level or benchmark. Different benchmarks may
   need to be applied under each of the headings of the FIRM Risk
   Scorecard. However, it is helpful if a single benchmark test for
   significance is applied.

2. **CASE**
   Acronym to assist with the definition and understanding of risk. A
   risk is and/or is associated with a "circumstance, action, situation
   or event" (CASE) with the potential to impact the mission of the
   organisation. In the narrowest sense, a risk has to be an event. The
   use of the acronym CASE will ensure that risks are accurately
   described and distinguished from management issues.

3. **Control Acceptance**
   The cost that the organisation accepts in order to achieve adequate
   management of control risks. Control Acceptance is the maximum
   expenditure that the organisation is willing to sanction to reduce
   the doubt and uncertainty associated with control risks to below
   the acceptable level.

4. **Control Risk**
   Type of risk with potential to cause doubt or uncertainty about the
   achievement of the mission of the organisation and/or the
   continuation of the core processes in the organisation. If the
   organisation removes or reduces the controls in place, there will be
   uncertainty about what will happen.

5. Core Process

A core process is fundamental to the continued success, or even existence in its present size and form, of the organisation and its ability to achieve the corporate mission. Each core process creates value in the organisation and delivers one or more stakeholder expectation. There are three types of core processes, as described in chapter 4.

6. Corporate Objective

Target or plan that must be fulfilled if the corporate mission is to be achieved. A full statement of objectives would set out the operational, change and strategic objectives of the organisation. It is possible to identify corporate objectives under each of the four headings of the FIRM Risk Scorecard.

7. Current Risk

The value of the risk that currently exists, taking into account the controls already in place. This should be compared with the inherent risk level. The greater the difference between the current level of risk and the inherent risk, the more effort and resources the organisation is putting into controlling that risk and the lower will be the scope for further improvement.

8. Financial Risk

FIRM Risk Scorecard heading that can be used to group the internal financial risks facing the organisation. Failure to adequately control these risks will be associated with weaknesses in the procedures within the organisation. Poor management of these risks will result in a procedures gap for the organisation.

9. FIRM Risk Scorecard

The headings used in the FIRM Risk Scorecard are:

F   Financial
I   Infrastructure
R   Reputational
M   Marketplace

The FIRM Risk Scorecard acts as a template for recording and illustrating the priority significant risk to the mission, corporate objectives, stakeholder expectations and the key dependencies.

10. **GRASP**

Acronym for the suggested future role of the risk manager. The
function of the risk manager should become:

G   Guardian of the

R   Risk

A   Architecture

S   Strategy and

P   Protocols

11. **Hazard Risk**

Type of risk with the potential to inhibit (and only inhibit)
achievement of the corporate mission of the organisation.
Hazard Risks can be considered to be threats or perils. These risks
are likely to be insurable risks.

12. **Hazard Tolerance**

Organisations will have a tolerance to the cost of hazard risks. The
total value at risk associated with this element of the overall risk
capacity of the organisation is the hazard tolerance. The hazard
tolerance is the maximum cost that the organisation is willing to
tolerate by way of losses from the hazard risks that it faces.

13. **Infrastructure Risk**

FIRM Risk Scorecard heading that can be used to group the internal
infrastructure risks facing the organisation. These risks are mainly
hazard risks and are closely related to insurable risks. Failure to
control these risks will result in poor performance of and/or
inefficiency in the core processes within the organisation. Poor
management of these risks will result in a process gap for the
organisation.

14. **Inherent Risk**

The value of the risk for the organisation before any controls are
applied. If there is a high inherent risk, the risk is likely to be
potentially significant, in the absence of any controls. Controls will
be needed before the risk can be considered to be under adequate
control.

15. **Key Dependency**

A key dependency is something that must be present to support a
core process. The key dependencies may be internal or external to
the organisation and may be tangible or intangible, financial or
non-financial. The FIRM Risk Scorecard is a useful structure for the

identification and recording of key dependencies associated with core processes.

16. Long Term Risk

5.1.3   79   A long term risk has the ability to impact the organisation some considerable time after the CASE occurred. Typically, the impact could occur between 1 and 5 years, or more, after the CASE has occurred. Long term risks impact the ability of the organisation to maintain the core processes that are designed to ensure future leadership of the market.

17. Marketplace Risk

5.2.4   88
9.1.2   155   The FIRM Risk Scorecard heading can be used to group the marketplace risks facing the organisation. These risks will be mainly commercial for organisations selling products. For other organisations, such as charities, these will be the risks related to the ability to raise funds in the marketplace. Failure to control these risks will result in inadequate sales or funds for the organisation in the marketplace. Poor management of these risks will result in a presence gap for the organisation in its operating marketplaces.

18. Medium Term Risk

5.1.2   79   A medium term risk has the ability to impact the organisation some time after the CASE occurred. Typically, the impact of a medium term risk would not be apparent immediately, but could be within 12 months of the CASE occurring. Medium term risks impact the ability of the organisation to maintain core processes that are designed to keep up with the competition.

19. Mission

4.1.1   61
9.1.1   154   The mission sets out the fundamental aim of the organisation. Typically, the mission will be brief and not contain too much detail. The mission should be an unambiguous statement of why the organisation exists and it implies what measurements will be used to determine the level of success that is achieved.

20. NUDE

1.2.1   12   Acronym for the desired state related to the control of hazard risks. The state that is required is one of:

N No
U Unplanned
D Dysfunctional
E Events

21. **Opportunity Appetite**

    Organisations will have an appetite for opportunity risks. 1.2.3   15
    Opportunity appetite is the maximum resource that the
    organisation is willing to put at risk to take advantage of perceived
    opportunities. Opportunity appetite is a component of the overall
    risk capacity of the organisation.

22. **Opportunity Risk**

    Type of risk with potential to enhance, although can also inhibit, 1.2.3   15
    the achievement of the corporate mission of the organisation. These 3.1.3   50
    risks are the risks associated with taking advantage of business
    opportunities. They are usually deliberately sought after and
    pursued by the organisation.

23. **Organisation**

    Any corporate, municipal, partnership, charitable or other body, 4.1   60
    set up to fulfil a mission, achieve corporate objectives and/or
    satisfy stakeholder expectations. The words corporate and
    organisation are used inter-changeably throughout this book.

24. **RAMS**

    Risk Assurance Management System.
    The application of risk management tools and techniques will be 2.1.7   31
    most successful if they are applied within a structure or standard, 7.1   120
    similar to the ISO 9000 set of standards applicable to quality 9.3   168
    assurance management systems. Chapter 9 sets out an approach
    that has all of the main features of a RAMS.

25. **RASP**

    Acronym for the risk architecture, strategy and protocols 7.1   120
    developed for the organisation. The RASP represents the 7.2   126
    administrative aspects of the overall risk assurance management 8.2   141
    system (RAMS) in place in the organisation.

26. **Reaction Planning**

    Stage 5 of the risk management discipline.
    Organisations need to decide how to react when a risk materialises. 2.1.5   30
    In the case of hazard risks, these plans will be referred to as disaster
    plans, recovery plans, or more commonly, as business continuity
    plans (BCP).

27. Reassurance of Control

Stage 3 of the risk management discipline
Adequate control of the significant risks is achieved when the current level of the risk is acceptable to the organisation. When risks are mature and/or under adequate control, further actions beyond stage 3 should not be necessary.

28. Reputational Risk

FIRM Risk Scorecard heading that can be used to group the risks to the reputation of the organisation. Failure to control these risks will result in an unsatisfactory image for the organisation. Poor management of these risks will result in a perception gap for the organisation in the marketplace.

29. Risk

A circumstance, action, situation or event (CASE) with the ability or potential to impact (inhibit, enhance or cause doubt) the key dependencies that support the core processes of the organisation. Core processes deliver the corporate mission of the organisation, at the same time as fulfilling corporate objectives and delivering stakeholder expectations.

30. Risk Assessment

Stages 1, 2 and 3 of the risk management discipline.
Risk Assessment is the combination of risk recognition, risk ranking and reassurance of control. The result of the risk assessment will be the risk profile for the organisation. Risk assessment can be undertaken for operations, projects and strategy, as discussed in chapter 2.

31. Risk Capacity

The risk capacity of the organisation is the maximum resource that the organisation is willing to put at risk. It should be agreed by the board and can be treated as a benchmark to evaluate the current risk exposure of the organisation. The component parts of risk capacity are:
- hazard tolerance;
- control acceptance; and
- opportunity appetite

32. Risk Exposure

The risk exposure for the organisation is the total value that the organisation currently has at risk. The risk exposure should be compared with the risk capacity to decide whether the organisation is taking more risk than the board is willing to accept. The risk exposure is the total of the individual current risk values. The total needs to be adjusted to take account of the extent to which the risks are correlated.

33. **Risk Guidelines**

The risk guidelines record the risk architecture, strategy and protocols (RASP) for the organisation. A statement of the risk management policy will be part of the risk guidelines. The purpose of the risk guidelines is to provide dynamic assistance with decision making in the organisation.

34. **Risk Management**

Risk management is a set of tools and techniques that build into an integrated robust discipline. The 7 stages involved in applying the risk management discipline are as follows:

1. Recognition or identification of risks
2. Ranking or evaluation of risks
3. Reassurance of control
4. Response to significant risks
5. Reaction planning or event management
6. Reporting and monitoring
7. Review of the RAMS

35. **Risk Matrix**

The risk matrix acts as an *aide memoir* to facilitate undertaking the risk assessment and producing the risk profile. The risk matrix facilitates the identification, recording and analysis of the key dependencies and the risks that could impact each of these dependencies.

36. **Risk Productivity**

Risk productivity is the concept that defines the contribution that can be made by risk management to the achievement of the mission for the organisation. The organisation should ensure that a cost effective return is achieved from the risk capacity of the organisation. All organisations should be making full use of the risk capacity of the organisation.

37. Risk Profile

Risk assessment is the consolidated outcome of stages 1, 2 and 3 of the risk management discipline. The risk profile is the record of the risk assessment. The risk profile may be recorded and presented as a risk register for the organisation, setting out details of the priority significant risks faced by the organisation.

38. Risk Ranking

Stage 2 of the risk management discipline.
Ranking or evaluation of risks in terms of magnitude and likelihood of the risk materialising at or above the benchmark level for significance. The aim of the risk ranking exercise is to compile an agreed list of the priority significant risks and thereby produce the risk profile for the organisation.

39. Risk Register

The risk register will contain details of the priority significant risks faced by the organisation. It defines and records the risk profile of the organisation. The risk register will contain details of the analysis of each of the priority significant risks, including details of the allocated risk productivity indicators (RPIs) that will be used to monitor risk performance.

40. Risk Recognition

Stage 1 of the risk management discipline
Recognition or identification of risks is the first stage in the management of risks. Using a risk matrix with the structure of the FIRM Risk Scorecard will assist in the identification or recognition of risks in a way that will reduce the danger of missing potentially significant risks, or producing too many risks in an unstructured format, leading to "risk overload".

41. Risk Reporting

Stage 6 of the risk management discipline
Reporting and monitoring of risk issues will be undertaken within the risk architecture of the organisation. Risk productivity indicators (RPIs) will be the main mechanism for monitoring the risk related performance of core processes. Risk reporting also includes the arrangements for reporting CASE and communicating risk information.

42. Risk Response

Stage 4 of the risk management discipline.

Following the identification of the priority significant risks during the risk assessment exercise, it is necessary to respond to the significant risks. Available responses include:

- accept or retain
- avoid or eliminate
- neutralise or hedge
- control or reduce
- insure or transfer

43. Risk Review

Stage 7 of the risk management discipline.

Review of the risk assurance management system (RAMS) on a periodic basis is essential. Risk review is a more structured stage in the risk management discipline than risk reporting and monitoring and will involve the board, possibly via the audit committee.

44. RPI

This is an acronym for risk productivity indicator.

The key performance indicators (KPIs) related to risks should be clearly labelled as risk based. The risk productivity indicators are these risk based KPIs.

45. Significant Risk

A risk is a significant risk if it could impact at or above the benchmark level for significance, applicable under the relevant heading of the FIRM Risk Scorecard. The benchmark level should be such that the risk would threaten the future existence of the organisation in its present size and form.

46. Short Term Risk

A short term risk has the ability to impact the continuity and efficiency of core processes. Short term risks cause dysfunction immediately the CASE occurs. They are predominantly hazard risks. These risks are associated with the achievement of NUDE and also with cost control in the organisation.

47. Stakeholder

All organisations have stakeholders and for most organisations, stakeholders will include at least the following:

- customers
- staff
- financiers and shareholders
- sponsors and suppliers
- pressure groups
- government

48. Stakeholder Expectation

Stakeholders will all have expectations of the organisation. A stakeholder expectation is a requirement that the stakeholder places on the organisation. Different sets of stakeholders may have contradictory, or even mutually exclusive, sets of expectations.

49. Turnbull

"Internal Control: Guidance for Directors on the Combined Code" (1999). Guidance for companies listed on the London Stock Exchange on the requirements relating to internal control. In particular, "the board should maintain a sound system of internal control to safeguard shareholders' investment and the company's assets".

50. Value at Risk

The value at risk for an individual risk is the corporate resource that is exposed by or allocated to the risk. The cumulative total of all values at risk is the risk exposure for the organisation. The risk exposure then needs to be adjusted to take account of the level of correlation of the risks that the organisation faces.

Appendix B

Consolidated Case Study

Explicit, structured and quantified management of risks facilitates achievement of the mission of the organisation

This extended case study demonstrates the contribution that structured and explicit risk management can make in the business world. Structured and explicit management of risks describes and defines the risk productivity approach that ensures the identification of the priority significant risks, so that appropriate measurements can be made to evaluate the level of control. This will enable an organisation to decide when a risk is being controlled at the optimum level.

These explicit measurements are the risk productivity indicators or RPIs. The use of RPIs will often be no more than re-labelling, as risk based, measurements that are already being undertaken as key performance indicators (KPIs). In other words, measurements previously taken as part of good management and implicitly as part of managing risks will now be taken explicitly as part of risk management. This will increase risk awareness and improve control of risks.

This case study uses all of the main ideas presented in this book to provide a consolidated description of the contribution that can be made by risk management to the achievement of the corporate mission. The intention is to:

1. Adopt an integrative approach

2. Ensure holistic assessment of risks

3. Align risk management with corporate mission

4. Embed actions within the organisation

1. Outline of Case Study

The case study considers a highly successful Premiership football team, Whitechapel Football Club (Whitechapel FC). The club is part of a larger hotel and leisure group, Whitechapel Lakes plc. The case study is concerned with Whitechapel FC only. Note that Whitechapel FC was used in the brief case studies in chapters 1 and 9.

Although expanding business interests have been built around the football ground, Whitechapel FC remains the most important business in a portfolio of compatible and mutually supportive businesses. The business activities of Whitechapel Lakes plc now extend to the following:

- Whitechapel Football Club
- WL Merchandising
- Whitechapel Club Catering
- The Chapel Hotel
- Whitechapel Travel
- Lakes Court Apartments

A new risk manager has been appointed, with the brief to introduce protocols for risk management to be aligned with the corporate mission, then embedded into normal management arrangements. The intention is to make full use and gain maximum benefit from the risk capacity of Whitechapel FC. The risk manager operates in a role of influence, co-ordination and persuasion only, without the support of a risk management department.

The risk productivity approach described in this book is to be applied to Whitechapel FC. The case study provides a simplified outline of the approach, outputs and benefits. The case study sets out the benefits that would be achieved and illustrates the impact of risk management and the risk manager on operational, project and strategic core processes.

This is not a fully worked case study. For example, the risk register is not presented in full and the risk architecture, strategy and protocols (RASP) are not documented. Enough information is presented to illustrate the nature and benefits of the approach.

Whitechapel FC is presumed to make profits of £40 million per annum and have a market capitalisation of £100 million. The benchmark values for a risk to be significant are 5% of profit (or an immediate impact of £2 million) and/or 10% of future earnings potential. This future earnings potential benchmark would be represented by a change of 10% in the share price or an anticipated future earnings impact of £10 million.

2. Twelve Steps to Risk Productivity

Although some of the steps suggested may seem complex and even burdensome, the outputs from these steps will prove to be very useful. As with a real organisation, the information required to undertake the work is readily available within Whitechapel FC. Part of the role of the new risk manager will be to locate the best source of the information that is required.

Figure 9 illustrates the twelve steps to achieving risk productivity. These twelve steps are divided into four phases. This case study demonstrates how these twelve steps can be applied in practice. The analyses presented throughout this case study are empirical in nature and provided for the sake of illustration only.

2.1 Whitechapel FC Mission

The mission sets out why Whitechapel FC exists and what it is seeking to achieve as a high level statement. The mission of Whitechapel FC is as follows:

To become a highly respected and internationally successful football club, with a world class football stadium, incorporating the finest club facilities in Britain.

2.2 Corporate Objectives

The corporate objectives for Whitechapel FC are a statement of the business imperatives for the organisation. These objectives have been established following the internal evaluation of Whitechapel FC. The objectives are entirely compatible with the corporate mission.

The main corporate objectives for Whitechapel FC are presented below, using the FIRM Risk Scorecard framework:

1. **Financial** – The main financial objectives are:
   - profit of 20% of gross income across all areas of activity
   - CapEx requests to incorporate an adequate risk assessment

2. **Infrastructure** – The main infrastructure objectives are:
   - facilities give rise to a customer satisfaction rating >99%
   - provision of world class standard of amenities

3. **Reputational** – The main reputational objectives are:
   - league position in the top three of the Premiership
   - Whitechapel FC remains internationally respected

4. **Marketplace** – The main marketplace (or commercial) objectives are:
   - average 90% utilisation of ground seating capacity
   - commercial activities of the club continue to diversify

Although these corporate objectives are useful, they are insufficient on their own to provide a full basis for the analysis of risks. The risks cannot be successfully identified at this stage, because there is insufficient information available about how these objectives will be delivered.

2.3   Stakeholders

There will be many stakeholders in Whitechapel FC, its mission and corporate objectives. Clearly, Whitechapel Lakes plc, as owners of Whitechapel FC, are an important stakeholder. The following are the other main stakeholders:

1. Supporters

2. Players

3. Staff

4. Financiers

5. Sponsors

6. Suppliers

Some of the stakeholder expectations will be reflected in the corporate objectives. However, a wider evaluation of stakeholder expectations will extend the range of issues covered. This will enable Whitechapel FC to establish appropriate core processes, designed to fulfil these stakeholder expectations.

2.4   Stakeholder Expectations

Table B1 sets out the expectations of the main groups of stakeholders in Whitechapel FC. There may be other stakeholders with additional expectations, although some of these will reinforce the expectations in Table B1. Note that some of the stakeholder expectations are contradictory.

	Stakeholder	Expectations
1.	Supporters	Sustained success on the pitch Inexpensive ticket prices Value for money food available in the ground Affordable range of merchandise News and information provided Simple and effective ticket booking arrangements Sufficient helpful and well trained staff Safe, clean and adequate facilities
2.	Players	World class coaching standards Excellent pay and conditions Fair team selection procedures Success on the pitch for the team Excellent physiotherapy provision
3.	Staff	Good pay and working conditions Adequate training and development Fair and equal employment practices Promotion and advancement prospects Pleasant and fun working environment
4.	Financiers	Publicity and sufficient visitor numbers Good management and reputation Appropriate income and profit Ethical behaviour by Whitechapel Football Club Good financial security and internal controls
5.	Sponsors	High profile brand publicity and exposure Fair and ethical behaviour by Whitechapel FC Safe, clean and adequate facilities Adequate marketing and visitor numbers Good publicity and positive reputation
6.	Suppliers	Prompt payment of moneys due to suppliers Fair and ethical treatment by Whitechapel FC Safe, clean and adequate facilities for franchisees Adequate marketing and visitor numbers Good publicity and positive reputation

Table B1: Stakeholder Expectations for the main stakeholders in WFC
Some expectations are contradictory, or even mutually exclusive

Table B1: Whitechapel FC Stakeholder Expectations

Analysing stakeholder expectations enables a common set of expectations to be identified. It is the job of management to respond to the competing stakeholder expectations and thereby give dynamic vision to the organisation.

2.5   Core Processes

A core process delivers one or more stakeholder expectation to the level decided by the organisation. Where stakeholders have differing expectations, the directors of Whitechapel FC will need to decide the level to which each core process will deliver these expectations.

Whitechapel FC will have core processes related to continuity and monitoring of routine operations; management of projects and enhancements; and development and delivery of strategy. The core processes for Whitechapel FC need to be discussed and agreed at board level. They are likely to include the following:

1.   Review opportunities and develop business propositions

2.   Obtain funding from financiers and/or shareholders

3.   Improve the stadium and its facilities

4.   Diversify distribution of matches (incl. Whitechapel TV)

5.   Ensure enjoyable match attendance experience

6.   Deliver successful results on the pitch

7.   Good selection of merchandise for football supporters

8.   Manage Whitechapel FC income and control expenditure

Figure B1 illustrates the level of expectation of each group of stakeholders in each of these core processes. Clearly all stakeholders have an interest in the overall success of Whitechapel FC, but not all stakeholders have the same stake in each core process. The darker colours represent higher expectations of that process by the particular group of stakeholders.

It is clear that some processes are more important than others. It is also clear that some processes have greater stakeholder expectations attached to them. Arguably, these are the core processes most at risk, in that failure of these processes would have the greatest impact overall on the ability to satisfy stakeholder expectations. From Figure B1, it is obvious that core process 6 *"deliver successful results on the pitch"* is the most important core process.

	Core Process							
Major Stakeholder	1.	2.	3.	4.	5.	6.	7.	8.
1. Supporters	10	10	70	70	100	100	70	10
2. Players	10	10	40	10	40	100	10	40
3. Staff	10	10	70	40	100	70	70	40
4. Financiers	70	100	40	70	40	40	40	100
5. Sponsors	70	70	10	70	70	100	100	40
6. Suppliers	10	40	10	70	70	70	70	40

The core processes for Whitechapel FC are as follows:
1. Review opportunities and develop business propositions
2. Obtain funding from financiers and/or shareholders
3. Improve the stadium and its facilities
4. Diversify distribution of matches (incl. Whitechapel TV)
5. Ensure enjoyable match attendance experience
6. Deliver successful results on the pitch
7. Good selection of merchandise for football supporters
8. Manage WFC income and control expenditure

Core Processes for Whitechapel Football Club
The darker colours illustrate greater stakeholder expectations

Figure B1: Core Processes for Whitechapel FC

2.6   Key Dependencies

For each of the core processes, the key dependencies can now be identified. Identifying key dependencies is a critical stage in the successful implementation of the risk productivity approach. The structure of the FIRM Risk Scorecard can be used to identify and record the key dependencies. This is likely to be undertaken during a brainstorming exercise.

Firstly the mission, followed by the corporate objectives, stakeholder expectations and each of the core processes in turn can be analysed to identify the key dependencies that support the management imperative under consideration. Table 7 in Chapter 9 sets out the partially populated risk matrix for Whitechapel FC. The risk matrix uses the headings of the FIRM Risk Scorecard as a means of grouping the key dependencies.

Each of the key dependencies will need to be carefully defined. For example, the key dependency stated as "Administrative and stadium staff" may be defined in more detail as "constant availability of an adequate number of suitably qualified and trained staff". The "The Stadium" key dependency may be defined in more detail as "stadium facilities and amenities that are sufficient to provide the required level of customer satisfaction".

2.7   Significant Risks

The identification of the significant risks is the second of the two brain storming exercises. Every circumstance, action, situation or event (CASE) with the ability to impact, inhibit, enhance or cause doubt to, the key dependencies, should be identified and placed in the most appropriate place in the risk matrix.

Although potentially time consuming, the reality is that the management and staff of Whitechapel FC will know or have access to all of the information that is required to populate the risk matrix. A common understanding of CASE will need to be established before population of the risk matrix can commence. This common understanding will ensure that the matrix is populated with risks, rather than setting out a list of the management issues facing Whitechapel FC.

Retaining the loyal support of fans is a high level management issue, or key dependency,) for Whitechapel FC, but it should not be labelled as a risk. It is the CASE that could impact this key dependency that should be considered to be the risks. The loyal support of fans could be impacted by:

- increase in ticket prices;
- loss of a key player;
- hooligan behaviour;
- unexpected defeat;
- etc

The identified risks can then be placed in the risk matrix under the most appropriate heading key dependency. As with the key dependencies, if a risk could impact two or more key dependencies, it should be placed in the risk matrix under the key dependency where the impact would be greatest. For the sake of illustration, Table 7 only analyses the top two key dependencies under each of the four FIRM Risk Scorecard headings. The risk matrix in Table 7 is not fully populated. It is likely that between 100 and 200, or more, risks will be included in the fully populated risk matrix.

2.8   Risk Priorities

Having fully populated the risk matrix, each of the risks must be evaluated in detail. The first stage is to ask which of the risks could impact above the defined benchmark test of significance. The benchmark values for significant risks are:

- 5% of profit, or an immediate impact of £2 million; and/or

- 10% change in share price for Whitechapel Lakes plc

These benchmarks can be applied to all potentially significant risks by asking whether the risk could impact by £2 million immediately, or impact the share price by 10%, representing a £10 million shift (positive or negative) in anticipated future earnings potential.

Having identified the potentially significant risks, the next stage is to determine the likelihood of each of these risks materialising at the significant level. This likelihood evaluation should take account of the controls that are currently in place. Indeed, both magnitude and likelihood are judged at the current level of risk.

In order to further develop the identification of risk priorities, consideration is given to the scope for further improvement in control. What emerges from this prioritisation procedure is a list of the priority significant risks. This approach has been described in Chapter 6. Figure 7 in Chapter 6 sets out a representation of the priority significant risks that have been identified by Whitechapel FC.

2.9   Analysis of Significant Risks

Each of the significant risks identified as a priority needs to be analysed in detail. The list of some of the significant priority risks for Whitechapel FC is set out in Table B2. The list shown is, in effect, the index page of the risk register. The main part of the risk register will be the page-by-page analysis of each risk, in accordance with the analysis suggested by Table 4 in Chapter 6. Table B2 lists the eight priority significant risks identified earlier in this case study.

For a risk to be significant it would have to impact one or more of the core processes within the organisation. Table B2 therefore identifies the core process that would be impacted and it also lists the owner of the core process and the owner of each significant risk. It is assumed that the owner of the risk will also be the owner of the key dependency that would be impacted.

Consider the risk that is currently stated as "adverse publicity associated with failure to comply with Listing Rules" (Risk R2). This is an example of a risk that can be hazard risk, control risk or opportunity risk, depending on the exact circumstances. Avoidance of adverse publicity is a hazard risk, seeking to tightly control all publicity represents a control risk and seeking to benefit from publicity makes the risk an opportunity risk. At the present level of maturity of the risk, Risk R2 is presented as a short term hazard risk because of the recent adverse publicity that affected the club and the potential for further unfavourable press coverage.

The detailed analysis of the priority significant risks will require a decision on whether the risk is under adequate control. It may be difficult to decide whether a risk is under adequate control, because it will not always be possible to precisely establish the required risk performance. Nevertheless, establishing the desired level of performance under each risk heading is necessary, so that risk productivity indicators (RPIs) can be assigned to each risk.

2.10 Risk Capacity

The benchmark test of significance for each individual risk will be indicative of the total risk capacity of the organisation. The risk capacity of the organisation is the maximum resource that the organisation is willing to put at risk. The risk exposure is the cumulative total of all values currently at risk. Figure 6 in Chapter 5 uses the Whitechapel FC data to illustrate overall risk capacity within the format of the FIRM Risk Scorecard. Figure 7 in Chapter 6 presents the information on the eight priority significant risks for Whitechapel FC, in a way that indicates the most appropriate response to each of these risks.

If each risk represents at least £2 million value at risk and there are eight priority significant risks, then it is likely that the total value at risk of Whitechapel FC is of the order of approx £30 million. Assume that the board has discussed the risk capacity of Whitechapel FC and decided that the current risk exposure of £30 million is appropriate and can be treated as the risk capacity of Whitechapel FC. Of course, the board would be free to decide that £30 million is too high or too low. In which case, steps would have to be taken to change the current level of risk exposure. The analysis offered in this case study does not include adjustment for correlation of risks, as discussed in Chapter 6.

For the sake of this case study, the following assumptions are made regarding the decisions of the board of Whitechapel FC:

1. The allocation of this risk capacity should be as follows:
    Hazard Tolerance   –   £8 Million
    Control Acceptance   –   £4 million
    Opportunity Appetite –   £18 million

2. The distribution of the risk capacity under the headings of the FIRM Risk Scorecard should be as follows:
    Financial Risks   –   £4 million
    Infrastructure Risks –   £7 million
    Reputational Risks   –   £4 million
    Marketplace Risks   –   £15 million

3. The individual priority significant risks total is £25 million and this is part of the total £30 million risk capacity. It is currently distributed as follows:
    Risk F1   –   £3 million
    Risk F2   –   £3 million
    Risk I1   –   £4 million
    Risk I2   –   £3 million
    Risk R1   –   £2 million
    Risk R2   –   £2 million
    Risk M1   –   £4 million
    Risk M2   –   £4 million

The overall value at risk is broadly in line with the agreed risk capacity of Whitechapel FC, bearing in mind that only eight of the risks are included above. The other significant risks will account for the remaining £5 million of risk capacity. Note that, although the actual total risk exposure is in line with the total risk capacity of Whitechapel

FC, it is not correctly distributed. There is currently too much risk under the Financial heading and too little under the Marketplace heading.

2.11 Response to Significant Risks

The data presented above is empirical, although it would not be difficult for Whitechapel FC to make reasonable judgements about the risk values. The important point is that this sort of risk valuation exercise is useful and can lead to decisions about the risk exposure and risk capacity of the organisation and the way in which the risk capacity is to be allocated.

Remember that risk is related to uncertainty and Whitechapel FC will want to achieve two important benefits at this time:

- firstly, the allocation of risk capacity needs to be reviewed and the benefits of re-distribution will need to be confirmed

- secondly, there needs to be benefits of reduced uncertainty arising from the application of risk productivity indicators to the priority significant risks

One of the conclusions is that Whitechapel FC has too much value at risk in relation to financial risks and so there is a need to reduce the values at risk related to internal financial control. This will make risk capacity available for opportunity risks in the marketplace, without putting Whitechapel FC in the position where the organisation is putting too much value at risk.

This additional marketplace risk capacity could be used for a number of purposes, including using the re-assigned risk capacity to:

- increase the value allocated to opportunity risk M1, by offering a wider range of merchandise to the supporters; or

- increase the value allocated to exploring the technology options associated with risk M2; or

- identify further marketplace opportunity risks and spread the risk portfolio for the organisation

2.12   Risk Productivity Indicators

Risk management is now contributing to the successful management of Whitechapel Football Club and the achievement of the corporate mission. The identification and allocation of risk productivity indicators (RPIs) will ensure that focused attention is paid to the management of the risks associated with the successful management of Whitechapel FC.

Risk productivity is a means of ensuring that full use is made of the available risk capacity. This will enable Whitechapel FC to pursue available opportunities to the full. The club needs to make arrangements to free some of the risk capacity being tied up in financial risks. This available risk capacity can then be used to pursue further opportunities. All of this can be done without increasing the risk exposure of the organisation.

The incorrect allocation of risk capacity in this case study needs to be addressed. Risks F1 and F2 need to be managed in a way that reduces the risk capacity allocated to these risks. Better control of these risks is necessary and this will be the responsibility of the owner of the key dependency that is impacted by the risk. The owner of the core process will also have a responsibility and in the case of both risks F1 and F2, that will be the finance director. The risk manager, head of internal audit and the audit committee all have responsibilities in respect of the need to reduce the values at risk associated with these financial risks.

The main point to be noted is that the actions agreed need to be monitored and the mechanism for monitoring these actions is the allocation of RPIs to the priority significant risks. This will encourage interested parties to agree the required risk performance and set appropriate RPIs. The reduction in the values at risk associated with risks F1 and F2 can then be monitored and the increase in values at risk associated with risks M1 and M2 can also be monitored.

3.   Risk Register

Table B2 sets out the summary information concerning the priority significant risks facing Whitechapel Football Club. For each of these priority significant risks, there will be a detailed page of analysis, as described in Table 4 in chapter 6. The summary page, together with the individual risk analysis pages form the risk register for Whitechapel FC.

Risk Index	Risk Title	Ownership of risk	Core Process	Ownership of Core Process
Priority Significant Financial Risks				
F1	Uncertainty about cost effectiveness of procurement strategy LT – Control Risk	Head of Procurement	Manage WFC income and control expenditure (Process 8)	Finance Director
F2	Unpredictable cash flow might cause short term cash shortages ST – Control Risk	Corporate Treasurer	Manage WFC income and control expenditure (Process 8)	Finance Director
Priority Significant Infrastructure Risks				
I1	Stadium Fire or other adverse and dangerous event during a match ST – Hazard Risk	Head of Security	Ensure enjoyable match attendance experience (Process 5)	Operations Director
I2	Uncertainty about the standard of training courses for staff MT – Control Risk	Head of Training	Ensure enjoyable match attendance experience (Process 5)	Operations Director
Priority Significant Reputational Risks				
R1	Match tactics designed to win matches and provide high entertainment LT – Opportunity Risk	Team Coach	Deliver successful results on the pitch (Process 6)	Director of Football
R2	Adverse publicity associated with failure to comply with Listing Rules ST – Hazard Risk	Company Secretary	Funding from financiers and shareholders (Process 2)	CEO
Priority Significant Marketplace Risks				
M1	Selection of merchandise that will be attractive to widest range of supporters LT – Opportunity Risk	Purchasing Consultants	Good selection of merchandise for football supporters (Process 7)	Commercial Director
M2	Uncertainty about the technology to be used for the launch of Whitechapel TV MT – Control Risk	Media Consultants	Diversify distribution of matches (incl. WTV) (Process 4)	CEO

Table B2: This shows the Index Page of the Risk Register for Whitechapel FC Allocation of RPIs will ensure monitoring of risk performance

Table B2: Risk Register for Whitechapel FC

Remember that the risk register is a snapshot in time of the risk profile of Whitechapel FC. It is the portfolio of the priority significant risks present at the time the risk assessment was undertaken. The risk register also forms an archive and audit trail of the priority significant risks. The registers will provide a history of each significant risk from the time the risk became a priority significant risk for Whitechapel FC, to the time that the risk was retired.

Risk management effort must not become too focused on the risk register. The production of a risk register is not the primary purpose of the risk productivity approach. Nevertheless, the risk register is a vitally important source of information for senior management and the audit committee.

The risk productivity approach leads to a position where risk management decisions become logical and well informed. The RPIs selected will have a fully justifiable rationale, both in terms of the RPIs selected and the level of risk performance, as indicated by the RPIs, that is required. The risk register summarises the information and explains and justifies the decisions. However, it is not the means of monitoring progress on a day-to-day basis. That monitoring is achieved by routine reports on the RPIs.

The relevant manager(s) will provide routine reports to the board member responsible for the appropriate core process. These will be the managers responsible for each priority significant risk that could impact a key dependency.

The risk register should also offer a means of identifying and monitoring emerging risks. This can be done by frequently updating the risk register and by setting out information in the risk guidelines on how the identification and subsequent management of emerging risks is to be undertaken.

Summary and Review of Case Study

Figure 9 sets out the twelve steps to risk productivity. This case study provides a structured description of how the twelve steps can be achieved in practice. The twelve steps are divided into four phases, as described overleaf. This summary presents a simple message relevant to each of these four phases.

Phase 1 – Organising for Risk Management
Trying to jump from a vague set of objectives to the identification of priority significant risks in a single step will not be successful, nor will it attract the full support of all interested parties.

Phase 2 – Evaluation of the Risk Environment
Whitechapel FC needs to clearly focus on the key dependencies that must be in place, so that the next stage of risk assessment will focus on the significant risks.

Phase 3 – Alignment of the Priority Significant Risks
Identification and detailed analysis of the priority significant risks in a robust manner will ensure that the management of these risks is aligned with the mission, corporate objectives and stakeholder expectations.

Phase 4 – Embedding Appropriate Actions
Appropriate actions have to be embedded into the normal activities and protocols of the organisation. There also needs to be an audit trail, so that decisions can be reviewed, as circumstances change.

The main message from this case study is that risk productivity has a contribution to make that is more wide-ranging than that which risk management has made in the past. If the high profile initiative that is risk management is to make a long term contribution to improved management of organisations, then there have to be demonstrable benefits. This case study points to what the benefits are and how they arise.